A TIME FOR VOICES

Books available by Brendan Kennelly

The Penguin Book of Irish Verse (Penguin, 1970; 2nd edition 1981)
The Boats Are Home (Gallery Press, 1980)
Cromwell (Beaver Row, 1983; Bloodaxe Books, 1987)
Moloney Up and At It (Mercier Press, 1984)
Mary (Aisling Press, 1987)
Landmarks of Irish Drama (Methuen, 1988)
Love of Ireland: Poems from the Irish (Mercier Press, 1989)
A Time for Voices: Selected Poems 1960-1990 (Bloodaxe Books, 1990)
Medea (Bloodaxe Books, 1991)
The Book of Judas (Bloodaxe Books, 1991)

BRENDAN KENNELLY

A Time for Voices

SELECTED POEMS 1960-1990

BLOODAXE BOOKS

ISBN: 1 85224 096 2   hardback edition
        1 85224 097 0   paperback edition
        1 85224 081 4   limited signed edition

First published 1990 by
Bloodaxe Books Ltd,
P.O. Box 1SN,
Newcastle upon Tyne NE99 1SN.

Bloodaxe Books Ltd acknowledges
the financial assistance of Northern Arts.

Second impression 1990.
Third impression 1991.

Typesetting by Bryan Williamson, Darwen, Lancashire.

Printed in Great Britain by
Billing & Sons Limited, Worcester.

For Kristen Kennelly

Acknowledgements

This book includes poems from the following collections by Brendan Kennelly: *Let Fall No Burning Leaf* (1963) and *My Dark Fathers* (1964), published by New Square Publications, Dublin; *Collection One: Getting Up Early* (1966), *Good Souls to Survive* (1967), *Dream of a Black Fox* (1968), *Selected Poems* (1969) and *Love Cry* (1972), published by Allen Figgis, Dublin; *Bread* (1971) and *Salvation, the Stranger* (1972), published by Tara Telephone Publications/Gallery Books, Dublin; *A Kind of Trust* (1975), *New and Selected Poems* (1976) and *The Boats Are Home* (1980), published by Gallery Press, Dublin; *Shelley in Dublin*, first published by Anna Livia Books/The Dublin Magazine Press in 1974 (and reissued in a re-written second edition by Beaver Row Press, Dublin, in 1982); *The Visitor* (St Beuno's Press, Dublin, 1978); *The House that Jack Didn't Build* (Beaver Row Press, 1982); *Selected Poems* (Kerrymount Publications, Dublin, 1985); and *Cromwell*, published in Ireland by Beaver Row Press in 1983 and in Britain by Bloodaxe Books in 1987.

Some of the uncollected poems first appeared in the *Irish Times*, *Massachusetts Review* and *Craft Review*.

Contents

FROM CROMWELL

Preface

I've tried to arrange these poems in an attempt to show the themes which I find most interesting and which I feel I can cope with in an interesting way. Broadly speaking, the structure of the book is chronological but this is not strictly adhered to because poems written years apart are often much closer in spirit than poems born very near each other. The same is true of families. These closenesses and affinities feel like accidents; yet, in the artificial symmetry of any "arrangement", they must be allowed to happen.

So I start with 'The Gift' (though poetry has to be earned through hard labour, it is essentially a given thing). I follow with 'The Blind Man' because that little poem is a white stick testing and prodding the air before me. We write out of our blindness; sometimes a poem becomes a shareable moment of light.

'The Story' I put next because behind everything I write is the story/ballad culture of my youth when a boy or girl had to be able to recite poetry and tell stories at the *Feis* (feast or celebration) before an audience. If the poem isn't shared it's not alive. Poetry should be consumed or it'll quickly become stale bread.

Many of my poems, including *Cromwell*, have a strong story element in them. We have little or no philosophical tradition in Ireland; reality is apprehended largely not through ideas but through stories. A man or a woman is a story. How to speak him, her? His history is his story. Whatever ideas we have come from our stories. When, recently, a man said to me 'I love great liars, they're the best company in the world' I knew what he meant; he was praising the makers of stories, the entertaining defiers of time. A good story puts a shape on the incomprehensible. Hence the magnetism of the 'liar'.

Next comes 'My Dark Fathers', about the Great Famine and its consequences, written twenty years before *Cromwell*. This is true of the way I write – it's a casual obsession born, in this case, of a conviction that the past is a savage educator, capable of defining the present with brutal precision; capable, too, of instilling murderous dynamism and butchering devotion into credulous minds and hearts. The quality of the education depends on who's telling the story. In *Cromwell* I try to let the story tell itself in all its bloody contradictions and bloody consistencies. Dark fathers have dark fathers with dark fathers with dark fathers...All were sons.

Then, there's a group of poems set in childhood, several of them fairly brutal or violent, naturally so, even the poems about the brutal teacher of religion. A man will beat the gentle Christ into children. A man with a stick, or a gun, is hot, or cold, with his own authority and truth. In the midst of that group I've placed 'Yes' and 'Entering', poems born of *positive* feeling *connected* with the brutality of the other poems.

Above all, poetry to me is *connection*, or the hope of connection both with oneself and with the outside world, with the living and the dead. The poem 'Connection' is placed after 'Dream of a Black Fox', which concerns dream-connection; and it precedes a group of poems in the first person – like the Old English riddles, whose beckoning, fugitive, vital voices I hadn't yet discovered (I hadn't read any apart from a small thing by Swift in that style).

This use of the first person is a great distancer from my point of view; by saying 'I' in such poems I experience a genuine sense of freedom, of liberating myself from my self. I have a terror of that sluggishness that wants to seduce/ambush us all into upright, respectable, "mature", competent corpses giving instructions to our youthful betters. I believe poetry must always be a flight from this deadening authoritative egotism and must find its voices in the byways, laneways, backyards, nooks and crannies of self. It is critics who talk of 'an authentic voice'; but a poet, living his uncertainties, is riddled with different voices, many of them in vicious conflict. The poem is the arena where these voices engage each other in open and hidden combat, and continue to do so until they are all heard. If there is 'an authentic voice' it is found in the atmosphere deliberately created so that the voices of uncertainties may speaksing their individual stories. The imagination, so often interpreted in terms of hierarchy, insists on its own democracy. This group ends with 'Silence' (what is the voice of silence?), and continues with 'May the Silence Break', a return to a more "direct" kind of poem, opening the way for a group of love poems, or love-hate poems, finishing with 'Keep in Touch' (why not?).

On then to 'Star' – about the cold fire of detachment. Then another poem *stating* something clear about poetry, the freedom/distance/readiness to eat oneself that makes it possible. 'Proof' is the name of that one – and it is followed by a group of such poems, ending with 'A Giving'.

This give-ness I perceive mostly in women, so there follows a celebration of this quality/state in a number of poems. I think, perhaps, that what I'm celebrating here is something I get from poems and people I love – an instructive radiance, an easy light-shedding, a weightless caressing of bewilderment into intensely lucid personal knowledge, a tenderising of rough frustrations, hastes, envies, calumnies, fatigues, futilities, felt on the skin of the body and the spirit.

Poems, then, about the city and its life: Dublin, noise, garrulous daylight and nightlight, chopping tongues, jokes, laughing invective, loneliness, the rush of unconsciousness and bellowing traffic, the black asses goaded by savagely punctual men. Madness, too, of the official variety, in 'A Visit'.

Over thirty years, one learns to mock oneself. A comic send-up of a good deal of the preceding material comes in 'The Sin'. 'Six of One', like 'The Sin', is about the roles of 'the savage ego'. 'Lear in Africa' follows, has to follow, here.

There follows a group of poems that will introduce a selection from *Cromwell*. All these have to do with forms of connection and disconnection, with inevitable attitudes of condescension and servility, exploitation and retaliation, cultivation and neglect, in the historical/political world, and appropriately introduce the Cromwell/Buffún drama of connection/disconnection.

This book deals with the notion that experience is a matter of bits and pieces, flickers, glimpses, fragments, things half-remembered, moments misrepresented; yet, by arranging it as I have done, I've tried to make it all of a piece. Why? Because if poetry is a giving, it should try to give a complete version of itself. Powerful figures such as The Visitor and Cromwell attract me because they act as if they were intensely *one* in themselves, dramatically and passionately present to themselves and to others, sure of their own voices, capable of uniting fragmented people about them. Poems try to do that. Poems that know how to surrender to experience can achieve a tyrannical capacity to master it. Much of the book concerns power – in love, religion, education, politics, work.

May I add that I have tried to "explain" my arrangement of these poems because I've distorted the order of their publication. When one distorts something one tries to say why.

BRENDAN KENNELLY

The Gift

It came slowly.
Afraid of insufficient self-content
Or some inherent weakness in itself
Small and hesitant
Like children at the tops of stairs
It came through shops, rooms, temples,
Streets, places that were badly-lit.
It was a gift that took me unawares
And I accepted it.

The Blind Man

Dark from birth,
And therefore spared the shock
Of losing light, not having known its worth.
I am aware of darkness round the clock,
A velvet kingdom, limits undefined,
Where touch, smell, ear equip me well.
Fastidiously, I try the noisy grind,
The aimless gusto of external hell.

I walk the inner alleys night and day,
Explore the salty laneways of the blood,
Note weeds and grasses, refuse thrown away,
Deduce what's evil, beautiful or good.
I move down sidestreets of the marrowbone,
Go moodily along its thoroughfare
On which the sun has sometimes shone;
And therefore I am blithe and debonair.

I've been informed of the things I miss:
Birds that steadily attempt the air,
Peculiar tints of whiskey in a glass,
Surprising sunlight in a woman's hair;
Shells half-buried in the sand
Originally spawned at sea,
Nature's gayest finery and
Casual phenomena of every day.

But vision is not simply seeing straight,
And things discoverable without exist within:
My shells and birds are different, yet elate
Me utterly. Images that spin
Within these limits are my own,
With colours, shapes and forms that I create,
Discovered somewhere in the blood and bone –
I only see whatever I can make.

Therefore I accept dark privacy;
I move beyond each voice
Which, unaware, asserts I cannot see.
While they acclaim, reproach, ignore, rejoice,
I go among them, prodding the strange air,
Awkwardly involved while still outside,
Conscious of the things I'm fit to share,
Acknowledging the light I've been denied.

The Story

The story was not born with Robbie Cox
Nor with his father
Nor his father's father
But farther back than any could remember.

Cox told the story
Over twelve nights of Christmas.
It was the story
Made Christmas real.
When it was done
The new year was in,
Made authentic by the story.
The old year was dead,
Buried by the story.
The man endured,
Deepened by the story.

When Cox died
The story died.
Nobody had time
To learn the story.
Christmas shrivelled,
The old year was dust,
The new year nothing special,
So much time to be endured.

The people withered.
This withering hardly troubled them.
The story was a dead crow in a wet field,
An abandoned house, a rag on a bush,
A sick whisper in a dying room,
The shaking gash of an old man's mouth
Breaking like burnt paper
Into black ashes the wind scatters,
People fleeing from famine.
Nobody has ever heard of them.
Nobody will ever speak for them.

I know the emptiness
Spread by the story's death.
This emptiness is in the roads
And in the fields,
In men's eyes and children's voices,
In summer nights when stars
Play like rabbits behind Cox's house,
House of the story
That once lived on lips
Like starlings startled from a tree,
Exploding in a sky of revelation,
Deliberate and free.

My Dark Fathers

My dark fathers lived the intolerable day
Committed always to the night of wrong,
Stiffened at the hearthstone, the woman lay,
Perished feet nailed to her man's breastbone.
Grim houses beckoned in the swelling gloom
Of Munster fields where the Atlantic night
Fettered the child within the pit of doom,
And everywhere a going down of light.

And yet upon the sandy Kerry shore
The woman once had danced at ebbing tide
Because she loved flute music – and still more
Because a lady wondered at the pride
Of one so humble. That was long before
The green plant withered by an evil chance;
When winds of hunger howled at every door
She heard the music dwindle and forgot the dance.

Such mercy as the wolf receives was hers
Whose dance became a rhythm in a grave,
Achieved beneath the thorny savage furze
That yellowed fiercely in a mountain cave.
Immune to pity, she, whose crime was love,
Crouched, shivered, searched the threatening sky,
Discovered ready signs, compelled to move
Her to her innocent appalling cry.

Skeletoned in darkness, my dark fathers lay
Unknown, and could not understand
The giant grief that trampled night and day,
The awful absence moping through the land.
Upon the headland, the encroaching sea
Left sand that hardened after tides of Spring,
No dancing feet disturbed its symmetry
And those who loved good music ceased to sing.

Since every moment of the clock
Accumulates to form a final name,
Since I am come of Kerry clay and rock,
I celebrate the darkness and the shame
That could compel a man to turn his face
Against the wall, withdrawn from light so strong
And undeceiving, spancelled in a place
Of unapplauding hands and broken song.

To Learn

There were nine fields between him and the school.
The first field was deep like his father's frown
The second was a nervous pony
The third a thistle with a purple crown
The fourth was a suspicious glance
The fifth rambled like a drinker's talk
The sixth was all wet treachery
The seventh was a man who did too much work
The eighth was downcast eyes, determined to be tame,
The ninth said hello, goodbye.
He thought of the nine fields in turn
As he beat the last ditch and came
In sight of the school on the gravelly rise.
He buckled down to learn.

The Stick

The man walked out of the classroom
And strode to the end of the yard
Where the ash tree was in bloom.
It was a calm day, the leaves barely stirred
As he searched the tree for the right strip.
He tried many pieces, threw them aside.
At last, he found the right size and shape
And with his knife sculpted
A thin hard stick, his work of art.
Back in the room, he looked at the boys' faces.
They'd be farmers, labourers, even singers, fiddlers, dancers.
He placed the stick on the mantlepiece above the fire.
His days were listening to boys' voices
Who'd know the stick if they didn't know the answers.

Catechism

Religion class. Mulcahy taught us God
While he heated his arse to a winter fire
Testing with his fingers the supple sallyrod.
'Explain the Immaculate Conception, Maguire,
And tell us then about the Mystical Blood.'
Maguire failed. Mulcahy covered the boy's head
With his satchel, shoved him stumbling among
The desks, lashed his bare legs until they bled.

'Who goes to hell, Dineen? Kane, what's a saint?
Doolin, what constitutes a mortal sin?
Flynn, what of the man who calls his brother a fool?'
Years killed raving questions. Kane stomped around Dublin
In policeman's boots. Flynn was afraid of himself.
Maguire did well out of whores in Liverpool.

After School

The teacher sneered, 'Carmody, I know you're dull
But try to answer.' Carmody's wild eyes
Floundered. 'Ah Carmody, you fool, you fool!'
The anguish in his face
Speared his heart. After school
The children badgered him beneath a bridge.
'Open his trousers! Quick! Pull out his tool!'
He stood there shivering on the edge

Of madness; their taunting fouled his ears,
Sent horror screaming through his mind.
Then amid the soul-insulting jeers
He heard the river at his side
Saying he should close his eyes on all his kind.
The river cried and cried and cried.

Killybegs

1

We drove across the mountains and the bog,
Magenta hypnotic in the fields.
To our left, a glacial lake black with cold
Dropped like a cracked abandoned shield.
You said, seeing a river, it was old:
The oldest river twists and turns at ease,
A proven legend casually re-told.
A younger river, hungry for the sea,

Cuts through the forest, clay and stone.
We watched the crooked meditative path
Sure of its future, glad to be alone.
Most of the time, sunlight is a wraith
In that land, always vanishing. Now
It sprinted through the mountain-range.
There was a change of gods above us. Below,
All the fields dazzled in golden change.

2

Killybegs. Evening. The Pier Bar.
Four old men drinking pints
Turn now and then to stare

At the sea. Up the blue creek
The boats come, rounding the red buoy.
Piratical bands of seagulls croak

Above the foam.
The boats bellies are heavy with fish.
The sea has given. The boats are home.

In piled boxes, the fish glint.
The sea's secrets
Are hauled towards a shed,

Hungry gulls following,
Cowards all
Till one whips a fish in his beak,

Veers out over the water
Where *Immortelle, Belle Marie*
And *Pursuit* lie at anchor.

The lone gull
Opens his jaws
Swallows the fish whole

Then turning from the pier he
Spreads his wings
For the open sea.

3

Back on the mountain road
The rain pelting.
Hard to see ten yards ahead.

This is a land of loss.
No sign of the river or the black lake.
Only roadside grasses toss and shake.

Even if we could see
There isn't a house for miles.

Suddenly there's a grey heap
In the road.
A mountainy sheep,

Its legs broken. No cry
As it tries to crawl to a ditch
Pushing grotesquely

With its furred back
Neat head
And nervous neck.

We can do nothing. The grey rain
Beats on nothing
But human helplessness and brute pain.

We drive on.
The sheep lies alone with its hurt.
The black clouds hang from the mountain.

Yes

I love the word
And hear its long struggle with no
Even in the bird's throat
And the budging crocus.
Some winter's night
I see it flood the faces
Of my friends, ripen their laughter
And plant early flowers in
Their conversation.

You will understand when I say
It is for me a morning word
Though it is older than the sea
And hisses in a way
That may have given
An example
To the serpent itself.
It is this ageless incipience
Whose influence is found
In the first and last pages of books,
In the grim skin of the affirmative battler
And in the voices of women
That constitutes the morning quality
Of yes.

                We have all
Thought what it must be like
Never to grow old,
The dreams of our elders have mythic endurance
Though their hearts are stilled
But the only agelessness
Is yes.
I am always beginning to appreciate
The agony from which it is born.
Clues from here and there
Suggest such agony is hard to bear
But is the shaping God
Of the word that we
Sometimes hear, and struggle to be.

The Brightest of All

The man who told me about the fall
Of the brightest of all the angels
Was Seán McCarthy
Who suffered badly from varicose veins
In the enormous cold classroom.
It wasn't always cold.
On certain days when the sun
Strode like All-Ireland victory into the room
Warming the windows the ceiling the floor
And the chipped desks where the boys
Sat in rows, devoted and docile
As slaves in a Roman galley
Arranged to cope with the sea
And no questions asked,
I thought of the brightest of all
Thrown out of home
Falling, falling
Down through the alien air.
People working the fields
Walking the streets of the cities
That were red circles and squares
On McCarthy's map of the world
Bluegreening a yellow wall
Gaped in wonder at brightness
That darkened the sun to a disc of shame
In the humbled sky.
In this piteous fabulous fall
The brightest of all
Crashed through the crust of the earth
Coming to rest
Deep in its secret heart.
When the scab fell away from the wound of the world
Healed in its own good time
The brightness was trapped in the secret heart
That sustains our birth
Accepts our death
And never complains or praises,
Patient and full of care

As my sister combing her rivery hair.
I was glad that the sun
Was no longer ashamed,
The people no longer dumb
At the sight of a shocking wonder.
And yet I was sad
That the brightest of all
Was trapped
And I thought
One gleam, one single gleam,
Not enough to shame the sun
But enough to brighten a man
May escape from the secret heart
Steal through the cold enormous classroom
Lessen the pain in McCarthy's legs
Where he stood
In the story of brightness expelled
From the painless kingdom
Of an angry God.
But the gleam never appeared.
Seán McCarthy's pain was no lie.
The secret heart is the deepest prison
Under the sky.

The Smell

The inside of the church absorbed the rain's thunder,
Lightning deceived and killed, the thunder never lied,
The thunder knelt and prayed at the high altar.
I was six years old. I knelt and prayed at her side.

She was a woman in black, she of the white head,
She whose lips rivalled the lips of the rain.
Someone closer to her than anyone had died far back.
That was the story. The story created her pain.

Out of her pain she prayed, always on her knees,
Her lips shaped secrets like rain in August grass.
Her white head, I knew, could not betray or deceive,
The thunder imitated the secrets of her heart.

I knelt at her side, my shoulder brushing her black,
Her lips surrendered visions of her private heaven and hell.
Drugged by her whispers, my head sank into her side,
My body and soul, in that instant, entered her smell,

Not merely the smell of her skin, but the smell
Of her prayers and pain, the smell of her long loss,
The smell of the years that had whitened her head,
That made her whisper to the pallid Christ on his cross,

The rent, dumb Christ, listener at the doors of the heart,
The pummelled Christ, the sea of human pain,
The sated Christ, the drinker of horrors,
The prisoner Christ, dungeoned in flesh and bone.

Her smell opened her locked world,
My closed eyes saw something of mine,
My small world swam in her infinite world
And did not drown but rose where the sun shone

On silence following the thunder's majestic prayer
For all the pain of all the living and dead,
I opened my eyes to the silence
Blessing her black clothes, her white head,

Blessing the smell that had told me something
Beyond lips' whispers and heart's prayer.
She took my hand in her hand, we moved together
Out of the church into the rain-cleaned air.

Horsechestnuts

Everything in the room was too clean.
The boy watched the old priest nod over his crossword.
The pencil slipped from his grip, rolled on the floor.
Once or twice, the boy felt he was smothering.
All the words flew off into the darkness
Like frightened birds whose wings obscured the stars.
The boy said goodnight to the old man's silence,
Picked his way in blackness between two lines of trees,
Horsechestnuts rising beneath him, crowding about him.
They were coming alive, soon their loneliness would cry out.
He started to kick them though he couldn't see.
He picked them up and threw them at the night.
These were men's hearts he was flinging about
As if the flinging might set them free.
He threw hearts at the darkness till he came
To the gate and the first shocking timid light.

Lost

To crawl away then from the shame or hurt
Or whatever it was
And to hide below the depths in your heart
Was all you could think of
Because the world was not only
Empty of love
But was a vast rat gnawing through concrete
To find your flesh.
So you took to a street
And entered a house

Emptier than yourself,
A raw place
Bleeding with memories
Of dawning and dying days.
And you knew

They'd be out in the roads looking for you
In no time at all,
Looking, looking for you
As though they needed assurance
You'd once existed
Beyond the shadowed edges of their lives,
Their voices calling your name
Falling like light rain
On your hurt or your shame
There in the cold of the old empty house,
Calling your name
To the road and the street and the air,
Calling with echoing care
To come out come back come home
From your sanctuary of dark and cold.
Was it minutes or hours or days
Before you came out?
Child in the light

You were found
And were never the same again.

Moving through each known face
You are often lost in the darkest place
Tasting the loss that is yours
Alone,
Hearing the voices call and cry
Come back come out come home
And you wonder why
Being lost in yourself should stir
This cry in others
Who seem together
Behind the shadowed edges of their lives,
Their own cries slashing the air
As the day dawns, as the day dies.

Entering

To be locked outside the image
Is to lose the legends
Resonant in the air
When the bells have stopped ringing.
If water soaks into the stone
And sunlight is permitted to caress
The worm and the root
And the feather lodged in the bird's flesh
Contributes to its flight

It is right
To enter the petal and the flame
Live in the singing throat
Mention a buried name
And learn the justice of the skeleton.

Entering,
I know that God is growth
In this garden of death.
I will always love the strangeness
And never be a stranger
In that thought
As I parry the shrivelling demons
And do my failing best
To rest
Among the flowing, growing forms
That open to my will,
Give access to their mercy
And share their skill.

The Exhibition

A girl hesitates under elm branches
Their shadows linking arms in the grass,
A few cobwebs depend on the logs of winter,
This tranquil cat suggests murderous ways,

A red setter shines across a road
To a child's muddy wellingtons thrown outside a door,
In a room of subdued music a woman
Fingers the gold in her hair

As if wondering whether to go on a spree
And spend every emotional coin
Or stay in that comfortable house
With himself and the children

Oh and a thousand other pictures
Are catalogued in my eyes.
I wanted to congratulate the artist
But he'd taken himself off down the sky

And was nowhere to be found.
Very soon, the show was over for the night.
I was grateful and decided to keep as a souvenir
My invitation printed in letters of light

Glowing more brightly in my head
The deeper my sleep.
My private collection is growing.
The more I give away the more I keep.

The Horse's Head

'Hold the horse's head,' the farmer said
To the boy loitering outside the pub.
'If you're willing to hold the horse's head
You'll earn a shilling.'

The boy took the reins, the farmer went inside,
The boy stood near the horse's head.

The horse's head was above the boy's head.
The boy looked up.
The sun attended the horse's head, a crown of light
Blinded the boy's eyes for a moment.

His eyes cleared and he saw the horse's head,
Eyes, ears, mane, wet
Nostrils, brown forehead splashed white,
Nervous lips,
Teeth moving on the bit.

The sun fussed over it.
The boy stared at it.
He reached up and gave the horse's head
A pat.

The horse's head shuddered, pulled on the reins,
Rasping the boy's hands, almost burning the skin,
Drawing blood to attention.
The boy's grip tightened on the reins,
Jerked the horse's head to order.
The boy was not afraid.
He would be master of the horse's head
Made of the sun
In the street outside the pub
Where the farmer stood drinking at the bar.

Daylight said the boy was praying
His head bowed before an altar.
The air itself became the prayer

Unsaid
Shared between the boy
And the horse's head.

The horse's head guarded the boy
Looking down from its great height.
If the boy should stumble
The horse's head would bear him up,
Raise him, as before,
To his human stature.

If he should lay his head against the horse's head –
Peace.

The farmer came out of the pub.
He gave the boy a shilling.
He led the horse away.
The boy stared at the horse.
He felt the reins in his hands
Now easy, now rasping,
And over his head, forever,
The horse's head
Between the earth and the sun.
He put the shilling in his pocket
And walked on.

The Grip

In Moynihan's meadow
The badger turned on the hound
And gripped.

The hound bit and tore
At the badger's body;
Harder, harder,
The badger gripped.

The men ran up.
O'Carroll shouted 'Quick! Quick! Crack a stick.'

The stick cracked.
Deceived,
The iron jaws relaxed.

The hurt hound bit in fury.
Again the badger
Gripped.
The neck, this time.

No loosening now.
Fangs tightened in a fierce embrace
Of vein and sinew.
No complex expertise, no difficult method,
No subtle undermining, no lying guile,

Only the simple savage style
As the hound weakened, slumped, died.
The white teeth parted
Red with the fresh blood.

The men watched him turn,
Head for a hedge,
Low grey killer,
Skin ripped from sides, back, head, neck.

O'Carroll prodded the dead hound
With a blackthorn stick,
Said, more to himself than to others
Standing there –

'A hundred hurts are bad
But a good grip
Will break the heart
Of the best hound in the land.'

The Tippler

Out of the clean bones
He tipples a hard music.
Cocking his head,
He knows himself sole master of his trade.
Hence his pride.

A goat ran wild
Through field and hillside,
Was tracked, caught, tethered, tamed,
Butchered and no man cried.
And the Tippler got his bones.

All bones dry in the sun,
Harden to browny white,
Mere flesh stripped and gone;
But bones create a new delight
When clacked by the proper man.

Let flesh lie rotten
When the Tippler takes his stand,
Holds the bones between his fingers;
Death has given him command,
Permitted him his hunger,

Made his heart articulate,
Tender, proud,
Clacking at shoulder, chest and head.
That man is for a while unbowed
Who brings music from the dead.

The Pig-Killer

On the scoured table, the pig lies
On its back, its legs held down
By Ned Gorman and Joe Dineen.
Over its throat, knife in hand, towers

Fitzmaurice, coatless, his face and hands
Brown as wet hay. He has travelled
Seven miles for this kill and now,
Eager to do a good job, examines

The prone bulk. Tenderly his fingers move
On the flabby neck, seeking the right spot
For the knife. Finding it, he leans
Nearer and nearer the waiting throat,

Expert fingers fondling flesh. Nodding then
To Gorman and Dineen, he raises the knife,
Begins to trace a line along the throat.
Slowly the line turns red, the first sign

Of blood appears, spreads shyly over the skin. The pig
Begins to scream. Fitzmaurice halts his blade
In the middle of the red line, lifts it slightly,
Plunges it eight inches deep

Into the pig. In a flash, the brown hands
Are red, and the pig's screams
Rise and fall with the leaping blood. The great heaving
Body relaxes for Gorman and Dineen.

Fitzmaurice stands back, lays his knife on
A window-sill, asks for hot water and soap.
Blade and hands he vigorously purges, then
Slipping on his battered coat,

Eyeing the pig, says with authority –
'Dead as a doornail! Still as a mouse!
There's a good winter's feedin' in that baishte!'
Fitzmaurice turns and strides into the house.

Time for the Knife

'You've a good one there,' Enright said.
Morrissey asked 'Is he right for cutting yet?'
Enright lifted the terrier pup in his fist
Slid the skin back on the gums
Fingered the neat fangs.

Caressing the brown and white head,
He handled the terrier's tail.

'Time for the knife,' he said.

The penknife from his waistcoat pocket
Flicked open. Twenty years of cutting tobacco
Had merely dented the blade.

'Let you hold the head.'
Morrissey gripped the skin behind the ears.

After he'd sharpened the knife on a stone
Enright stretched the tail
And started to cut.

It was over soon. Enright looked
At the severed tail in his fist
And pitched it into the grass.

The terrier pup
Howled as it fled,
Pursued by drops of its own blood
Regular as a pulse of pain.

For a while
It whimpered and cried alone
Like a woman mourning.

When the bleeding stopped
The stubby tail stuck up
Like a blunt warning.

The Stones

Worried mothers bawled her name
To call wild children from their games.

'Nellie Mulcahy! Nellie Mulcahy!
If ye don't come home,
She'll carry ye off in her big black bag.'

Her name was fear and fear begat obedience,
But one day she made a real appearance –
A harmless hag with a bag on her back.
When the children heard, they gathered together
And in a trice were
Stalking the little weary traveller –
Ten, twenty, thirty, forty.
Numbers gave them courage
Though, had they known it,
Nellie was more timid by far
Than the timidest there.
Once or twice, she turned to look
At the bravado-swollen pack.
Slowly the chant began –

'Nellie Mulcahy! Nellie Mulcahy!
Wicked old woman! Wicked old woman!'

One child threw a stone.
Another did likewise.
Soon the little monsters
Were furiously stoning her
Whose name was fear.
When she fell bleeding to the ground,
Whimpering like a beaten pup,
Even then they didn't give up
But pelted her like mad.

Suddenly they stopped, looked at
Each other, then at Nellie, lying
On the ground, shivering.

Slowly they withdrew
One by one.

Silence. Silence.
All the stones were thrown.

Between the hedges of their guilt
Cain-children shambled home.

Alone,
She dragged herself up,
Crying in small half-uttered moans,
Limped away across the land,
Black bag on her back,
Agony racking her bones.

Between her and the children,
Like hideous forms of fear –
The stones.

Innocent

Only the innocent can be total monster.
Myles Bartishel, bored at seven years old,
Scoured holes and crevices for hungry spiders
But found none. Thwarted and blackening, he held
His patience but didn't change when the sun
Emerged, kind as a father, to throw its light
On the spiderless world. Myles turned to a pane
Of glass, warm to the touch. On its face a fly

Moved as if it wanted to pierce the glass
And flit forever in that blue infinity
Of cool reflection and intangible things.
He let it flounder; then got it between his
Fingers. Two tugs. On the ground, the fly's body
Jerked. Myles held in his hand two silver wings.

Poem from a Three Year Old

And will the flowers die?

And will the people die?

And every day do you grow old, do I
grow old, no I'm not old, do
flowers grow old?

Old things – do you throw them out?

Do you throw old people out?

And how you know a flower that's old?

The petals fall, the petals fall from flowers,
and do the petals fall from people too,
every day more petals fall until the
floor where I would like to play I
want to play is covered with old
flowers and people all the same
together lying there with petals fallen
on the dirty floor I want to play
the floor you come and sweep
with the huge broom.

The dirt you sweep, what happens that,
what happens all the dirt you sweep
from flowers and people, what
happens all the dirt? Is all the
dirt what's left of flowers and
people, all the dirt there in a
heap under the huge broom that
sweeps everything away?

Why you work so hard, why brush
and sweep to make a heap of dirt?
And who will bring new flowers?
And who will bring new people? Who will
bring new flowers to put in water
where no petals fall on to the

floor where I would like to
play? Who will bring new flowers
that will not hang their heads
like tired old people wanting sleep?
Who will bring new flowers that
do not split and shrivel every
day? And if we have new flowers,
will we have new people too to
keep the flowers alive and give
them water?

And will the new young flowers die?

And will the new young people die?

And why?

The Visitor

He strutted into the house.

Laughing
He walked over to the woman
Stuck a kiss in her face.

He wore gloves.
He had fur on his coat.
He was the most confident man in the world.
He liked his own wit.

Turning his attention to the children
He patted each one on the head.
They are healthy but a bit shy, he said.
They'll make fine men and women, he said.

The children looked up at him.
He was still laughing.

He was so confident
They could not find the word for it.
He was so elegant
He was more terrifying than the giants of night.

The world
Could only go on its knees before him.
The kissed woman
Was expected to adore him.

It seemed she did.

I'll eat now, he said,
Nothing elaborate, just something simple and quick –
Rashers, eggs, sausages, tomatoes
And a few nice lightly-buttered slices
Of your very own
Home-made brown
Bread.
O you dear woman, can't you see
My tongue is hanging out
For a pot of your delicious tea.
No other woman in this world
Can cook so well for me.

I'm always touched by your modest mastery!

He sat at table like a king.
He ate between bursts of laughter.
He was a great philosopher,
Wise, able to advise,
Solving the world between mouthfuls.
The woman hovered about him.
The children stared at his vital head.
He had robbed them of every word they had.
Please have some more food, the woman said.
He ate, he laughed, he joked,
He knew the world, his plate was clean
As Jack Spratt's in the funny poem,
He was a handsome wolfman,
More gifted than anyone
The woman and children of that house
Had ever seen or known.

He was the storm they listened to at night
Huddled together in bed
He was what laid the woman low
With the killing pain in her head
He was the threat in the high tide
At the back of the house
He was a huge knock on the door
In a moment of peace
He was a hound's neck leaning
Into the kill
He was a hawk of heaven stooping
To fulfil its will
He was the sentence tired writers of gospel
Prayed God to write
He was a black explosion of starlings
Out of a November tree
He was a plan that worked
In a climate of self-delight
He was all the voices
Of the sea.

My time is up, he said,
I must go now.

Taking his coat, gloves, philosophy, laughter, wit,
He prepared to leave.
He kissed the woman again.
He smiled down on the children.
He walked out of the house.
The children looked at each other.
The woman looked at the chair.
The chair was a throne
Bereft of its king, its visitor.

Baby

I find it interesting to be dead.
I drift out here, released, looking down
At men and women passing judgement
In the streets of that moneymad little town.
I enjoy the jokes about me, scribbled in the Gents,
I like the lads in suits, their smart legal faces,
I follow them through every argument,
I note their gas antics at the Listowel Races.
There was a hope of love at the back of it all
And in spite of clever men making money
That small hope still survives.
Will I name the clever men for you? Yerra, no.
I smile to watch them prospering to their ends
But thanks be to Jesus I won't have to live their lives.

They're trying to find out who killed me,
A fascinating exercise.
If I were water I'd let them spill me
And I'd run out of their eyes.
If I were fire I'd burn books of law
And half-burn the men who study them.
If I were air I'd slip into their lungs
And out of pity revive them.
If I were earth – O now that I think of it
That's what I am or am becoming
A little more quickly than you, and painlessly.
Tell me what you think it means to be alive,
I'd love you on that topic, expounding.
Being dead, I must find out, you see.

And yet, being dead, I may grow
To be a small, cheeky flower
Peeping through a veil of snow
On the scarred face of the earth
That never grows ashamed;
Or I may be
A blade of grass to nourish you;
Or a book

Wherein the nosey world may read
Of lovers' luck
And what it means to bleed.

When I was being formed in her body
I could tell she was kind.
My toes my fingers my eyes
My hands my bum my tiny mind
Knew that.
She carried me everywhere.
I couldn't see where I was going.
She did.

Streets, roads, fields, kitchens,
Bedrooms, chapels, small hotels, fish and chip places,
Glances of men in cars, glances
Of women both barren and fulfilled –
I'm buried now under the strong feet
Of money. I'm dead. I hope my mother
Sings and dances.

Girl on a Tightrope

They've set up the tent in the blacksmith's field
And the village children
Stare at the girl on the tightrope
As if they were astronauts
Staring at the world
Like men on the first morning of creation
Seeing mountains valleys rivers lakes
In colours never seen before

While down below
A clown grins
A greasy grin
And prepares to ride a horse

Around the ring
In the tent
In the blacksmith's field
Where the world begins

She is stepping a line
The children have never known
Somewhere between earth and sky
Somewhere they have never been

A line of danger and adventure
A line of longing and of love
A line of breathing and of breathlessness
A line of poised humanity and vigilant divinity

In the tent in the blacksmith's field
With the children watching

She is stepping there
Between girl and goddess
And her hair is black and tight
And bound with a ribbon of light
At the back of her head
Neat as a bird's

And the light of eyes is on her
Guiding her
Willing her
To move safely in her silence

Billy O'Sullivan is praying for her
And Tony Crow is begging God to bring her safe
And Martha Kane's lips freeze in terror
And Tommy Doran's mouth is an o of awe
And Mona Coleman's hands are locked together
And Danny Dalton shuts his eyes
More tightly than ever he shut them before
But he cannot shut her out
He cannot shut her out

For she is there
On a line in the air

With a ribbon of light in her hair
Looking neither up nor down
But straight ahead
As though there were a road in the air
With fields on either side
She will look at later
Or even enter
For a moment's rest
After a journey through her own silence
And the children's silence
And their riveted eyes
On legs hands body head
Neat as a bird's

O if only she could fly
There would be no danger then
That she might fall and die

But she steps her way
To where she must go
And she will reach that spot
And smile
And wave
At children happy in her moving
And arriving

Children clapping stamping shouting
Till they're hoarse

And the lumpy clown
Grins
A greasy grin
Tries
And fails
To ride a horse

Around the ring
In the tent
In the blacksmith's field

Where the world begins

Love-Cry

He mounted her, growing between her thighs.
A mile away, the Shannon swelled and thrust
Into the sea, ignoring the gaunt curlew-cries.
Near where the children played in gathering dusk
John Martin Connor cocked his polished gun
And fired at plover over Nolan's hill;
A second late, he shot the dying sun
And swore at such an unrewarding kill.

A quick voice called, one child turned and ran,
Somewhere in Brandon's river a trout leaped,
Infinite circles made nightspirits stare;
The hunter tensed, the birds approached again
As though they had a binding tryst to keep.
Her love-cry thrilled and perished on the air.

The Thatcher

He whittled scallops for a hardy thatch,
His palm and fingers hard as the bog oak.
You'd see him of an evening, crouched
Under a tree, testing a branch. If it broke
He grunted in contempt and flung it away,
But if it stood the stretch, his sunken blue
Eyes briefly smiled. Then with his long knife he
Chipped, slashed, pointed. The pile of scallops grew.

Astride a house on a promised day,
He rammed and patted scallops into place
Though wind cut his eyes till he seemed to weep.
Like a god after making a world, his face
Grave with the secret, he'd stare and say –
'Let the wind rip and the rain pelt. This'll keep.'

The Swimmer

For him the Shannon opens
Like a woman.
He has stepped over the stones

And cut the water
With his body
But this river does not bleed for

Any man. How easily
He mounts the waves, riding them
As though they

Whispered subtle invitations to his skin,
Conspiring with the sun
To offer him

A white, wet rhythm. The deep beneath
Gives full support
To the marriage of wave and heart.

The waves he breaks turn back to starc
At the repeated ceremony
And the hills of Clare

Witness the fluent weddings
The flawless congregation
The choiring foam that sings

To limbs which must, once more,
Rising and falling in the sun,
Return to shore.

Again he walks upon the stones,
A new music in his heart,
A river in his bones

Flowing forever through his head
Private as a grave
Or as the bridal bed.

The Runner

The truest poetry lies
Just now
On a runner's rainy thighs

While at his head
White rings of breath
Break with his stride.

Winter trees, the windy cries
Of seabirds blown inland
Are witness

To every move he makes.
I wish him well
Whatever barriers he breaks.

He runs towards a freedom
Desired by every man
But always there, ahead of him,

Freedom runs on swifter feet.
He runs with the joy of losing
Yet plucks a sweet

Gift from the air.
When he stops
The gift's no longer there.

I think that in his mind
He runs forever
Out of the green field. Now he is blind

With joy, striding a mountain path,
A morning beach
Hard from the sea's creative wrath,

A heavy suburb, a country road
Where rough welcome
Lives in his blood.

Yet even there, or anywhere,
He runs to lose.
On the winter air

Nothing can be seen
But fragile rings of white
Breaking on the green.

bridge

and in the dark to lean across
like a bridge over a river on whose bed
stones are untroubled by what passes
overhead
and kiss the sleep in your body
with I love you I love you
like currents through my head
that is closer to deep water now
than at any time of the day

The Kiss

'Go down to the room and kiss him,
There's not much left o' him in the bed.
He had a good run of it, over eighty years.
In a few days he'll be dead.'

My nine years shook at the words 'kiss him'.
I knew the old man was something to my father.
I knew I had to do what my father said.
I trembled to the bedroom door

And entered the room where the drawn curtains
Foiled the light.
Jack Boland was a white wreck on the pillows,
His body a slight

Hump under the eiderdown quilt, starred white and red,
Everything under the black crucifix
With gaping mouth and bleeding head.
He saw me, half-lifted a hand. 'Here, boy,' he said.

I walked across the bedroom floor
And felt the ice in his hands enter mine.
His eyes were screwed up with sickness, his hair was wet,
His tongue hung, slapped back. Every bone

In my body chilled as I bent my head
To the smell and feel of the sickspittle on his lips.
I kissed him, I find it hard to say what I kissed
But I drank him into me when I kissed him.

I recognised something of what in him was ending,
Of what in me had scarcely begun.
He seemed without fear, I think I gave him nothing,
He told me something of what it is to be alone.

There is no way to say good-bye to the dying.
Jack Boland said 'G'wan, boy! Go now.'
I shivered away from his hands, his smell,
The wet blobs of pain on hair and brow,

The weak, eager touch. My childfear
Went with me out into the corridor, stayed
Inside me till I stood again at my father's side,
Head down, thinking I was no longer afraid

Yet feeling still the deathlips rummaging at my lips,
The breath a sick warmth mingling with my breath.
It's thirty years since I bent my head to the kiss.
Ten thirties would not make me forget.

The Hurt

Jack Ahern was gored by a bull
One day in deep winter.
He was sixty-two. For three years after he sat silent
Staring into the fire,

Graffa turf stacked brown and black
Reddening in the hearth, reddening in his eyes.
He stared at fire, a man of fire
Turning the colour of ashes.

Every night of these dying years
He washed his feet
In a chipped enamel basin,
The flesh dark and white by firelight.

The bull had mauled his breast.
His hand hovered at his heart
As if seeking to touch it.
All he ever found was the hurt

Rending his body that had worked the fields
And rarely been ill.
Now he read in the fire's eyes
How he'd never be well

Till the grave released him
From pain so unshareably his own
Daylight was a gulf
Between him and everyone.

There was a fire with its own life
Never the same from second to second,
There was a man trying to understand
Why this hurt had happened

On a darkening winter afternoon
In his favourite meadow.
He'd cut hay there for forty years
And not suspected his sorrow

Waited its proper moment.
Were all his days a waiting for this?
Why, when he tried to see,
Did his heart know the world was

A Hereford bull horning the air
In its red rush
To pile on a tiring man,
Mangle his flesh,

Roar off like a winter storm
On its blind way,
Not knowing what it had broken,
What lay

Bleeding and gasping on the grass
Where love was willing to work
Till horns and hooves
Pounded it into the muck

And it was borne in pain by other men back into the house
To rest but not recover, between bed and chair,
Seeing the infinite shapes of hurt reach out,
Recede, renew themselves in eyes, in fire.

That Look

Jack Scanlon heard the scrape at the back door.
The rat was in the yard outside.
He went out front, untied the wire terrier,
Opened the back door, gave the dog his head.
The scraping stopped, no sound for a while,
A tension grew, the snarling started then,
A throaty menace hard and full.
Scanlon stepped into the sun,
Saw the rat cornered near a wall,
The terrier crouched, head down, fangs clean
As knives in the light. Scanlon moved three paces
As if to give command. With a growl
The terrier killed the fear and hate in
The rat's eyes. I've seen that look in people's faces.

A Leather Apron

After he cut the lamb's throat
He held it out from him by the hind legs
And let it kick for a minute or so.
Then he laid it on the table
That was hacked and scarred like a few faces
I've glimpsed in streets. Slowly then he drew
The bleeding knife across the leather apron
Covering his belly.

       I saw the lamb's blood
Wiped from the knife into the leather,
From the leather through the clothes, through the skin
Until it lived again in every butchering vein.
Unless he absorbed what he killed, I'll never
Tell the gentling touch of the man.

A Man in Smoke Remembered

A man in smoke remembered
Lifts his head
From the silence of the dead
And here, beside a fire
Packed to battle a winter,
Lifts a hammer
Takes a tack from between his lips
Thumbs it into place in the cut leather
And beats it home.

What is memory but cutting through smoke?
How well did I know him living?
He lives now, real as rock
In my mind.
His grey head chuckles through smoke
His stories stand up and laugh in smoke
His words are small bright nails
Lit by flames
Dancing in the corner of a smokey room.

He will die alone in a home for the old.
In a garden
Which he chooses to ignore
He sits on a green bench
Glad of a noggin of whiskey.

Leaving the whole crowd behind
Was not as bad a wrench
As he'd imagined it might be,
But he doesn't like the other old people
And complains that they complain too much
Especially of callous families
Who take care of themselves alone
And know how to forget
Long summers, long winters
That put them in an old man's debt.

He will chuckle to the end
And fiercely scratch his head when brooding.
This is the last time I'll see my friend
Until I see him in smoke
Twenty years through the fire.
Again it is winter
And he is chuckling
With more self-delight than ever.
He sits across the hearth from me
For an hour, the smoke
Weaving its own stories around his head.
He rises then and shuffles back to the dead.

A Man, But Rarely Mentioned

They spoke more about the killing frost
Of January than of him.
Every tongue was dumb
When it came to mentioning his name.
The road of agreed silence
Led to oblivion.

Con. Con.

The boy tasted the sad
Syllable in the dark
Until the word was a pool
Where he cooled his fevered mind.
The pool formed from a shy river
Among stones in high ground,
Legends of drownings
Grew like grass at its edges,
Dark stones like unblinking eyes
Stared from the depths,
Revealing nothing.

But the boy knew it was there
He must go for news of the man
Who was rarely mentioned
And then so briefly
He might not have been mentioned at all.

The boy stared at the pool
And said Con, Con,
Until the man
Smiled from a stone
In the middle of the pool
Saying 'Only a loving fool
Chooses to know what is so forgotten
And not, perhaps, without reason
When one considers the stones of fear
Hurled at men and women.
There are worse things than the repose
Of being ignored
Though why this is so, nobody knows
And nobody should know.
I will live in some corner of your mind
Wherever you go.'

The boy took the stone's word with him
Away from the pool,
Something that had been completely dumb
Was no longer completely dumb.
One sad syllable had spoken.
One chain of wrong was broken.

The Gift Returned

He was at the front on the right.
He could hear his brothers' breathing.
He could feel Jack's tight
Grip on his right shoulder. She'd said

'My death will teach you brotherhood.
There will be nobody younger, nobody older,
There will be brothers giving my death back
To the living grass.
The earth is crying out for us
And cares nothing for our grief.
When you bear me from this house
Where, on a fine day, from this hill I could see
Five counties and three rivers,
You will be farther from me
And nearer to each other
Than ever before.
All I know of dying
Tells me it is a tearing
Leading to new binding.
Wash my body
Before you give it back.'

Now, returning her to herself, they bore
Her washed corpse across the stony yard
Where she'd worked for seventy years
And he knew, feeling his brother's fingers
Cut for support into his shoulder
As though he were a drowning man,
Her deadweight was the lightest thing imaginable
To bear for a lifetime in his mind,
Making him adore the distance
That was the love between him and his kind.

Two five-bar gates between them and the road,
The people a black muttering sea,
The brothers four moving pillars
Bearing something familiar and incomprehensible
Over the stones
To the place of skulls and bones,
Small crooked roads ahead
Puzzling the hedges,
Supporting the living and dead
With earth's unkillable courtesy.
They shuffled through silent light
Becoming one under the weight
Of what had lived to be returned

To a deeper love
Than any moving man could ever imagine.

Yet it was there in the patient grass,
In her final silence,
In his brothers' breathing,
In the place authentic beyond words
Where the sense of returning
Swallowed the sense of leaving.

A Beetle's Back
(for Margaret McAnallen)

People are distant but the gods are near
And a beetle's back is nearer than any god.
Here among stone are those who live in colour:
Green black yellow blue purple red.

An hour ago my words admitted defeat
And showed the white flag of surrender.
The colours took the flag, tore it asunder
And dropped the pieces in the harbour water.

Seeking to make warm this feeling of defeat
I walked the by-roads without light.
There were holes deeper than shame or fear
And there was a beetle's back to comfort me,
A shiny black back, anonymous and exquisite,
Making the people distant, the gods near.

Whatever I forget I know what I'll remember
From hours of stone and walk and word and colour:
Hyacinth mauve ochre grey –
Not even the colours know what the colours say.

The Learning

The learning goes on forever.
A pigeon dozing in the ivy
Is sending out bulletins
I am trying to decipher.

The streets survive, offering their thoughts
At no cost. Lost
Rivers plead under our feet,
Astray in themselves,
Sharing our anonymity.

With what devotion
The children of ignorance
Apply themselves to learn
The streets' wisdom, the rivers' rhythms
In the spell of the flesh
Failing through self-repeating evenings.

Listen!
Is it a bomb or a heart-beat?
A tired sigh of the past
Or the future's optimistic eye?
Touch of some habitual defeat?
The sound of a kiss
That cannot be returned
Though all our lives
We have yearned, we have yearned.

I will spend what I have to spend
And never accuse my pockets of time
Of hoarding or squandering, getting or shedding
Possessions.

It is as though I were straining to hear
Low, happy laughter
Vanishing in the grass of an occupied garden
One summer evening
That lays itself down

Like a cat in the corner of a shed
After taking its prey
That lost day.
It rests now, sweetly surfeited
While round the corner of the hour
Hunger waits like the bad news
We fear to hear.

The spending burns on.
I will always turn to this burning
As the days
To the repeated losing of themselves,
Throwing themselves away as though
They could not bear the burden of themselves
That must come again as they happened long ago,
Each one a child, a corpse, a proven fighter

In the learning that goes on forever.

Dream of a Black Fox

The black fox loped out of the hills
And circled for several hours,
Eyes bright with menace, teeth
White in the light, tail dragging the ground.
The woman in my arms cringed with fear,
Collapsed crying, her head hurting my neck.
She became dumb fear.

The black fox, big as a pony,
Circled and circled,
Whimsical executioner,
Torment dripping like saliva from its jaws.
Too afraid to show my fear,
I watched it as it circled;
Then it leaped across me
Its great black body breaking the air,
Landing on a wall above my head.

Turning then, it looked at me.

And I saw it was magnificent,
Ruling the darkness, lord of its element,
Scorning all who are afraid,
Seeming even to smile
At human pettiness and fear.

The woman in my arms looked up
At this lord of darkness
And as quickly hid her head again.
Then the fox turned and was gone
Leaving us with fear
And safety –
Every usual illusion.

Quiet now, no longer trembling,
She lay in my arms,
Still as a sleeping child.

I knew I had seen fear,
Fear dispelled by what makes fear
A part of pure creation.
It might have taught me
Mastery of myself,
Dominion over death,
But was content to leap
With ease and majesty
Across the valleys and the hills of sleep.

Connection

Self knows that self is not enough.
The deepest well becomes exhausted.
We could wander forever in a wood
And through the trees not see a sign of love.
Turn then where windy March blows golden hair
(A drowning man will grasp the thinnest straw)
And slowly in the ceremonious air
Observe irrational redeeming law

Connect the desert with the sun at noon
Revealing open beaks, descending wings
And bones that hint of spirits that are free.
We open in a moment, love, and then
Linked with the livingness of growing things
Express the shell and comprehend the sea.

The Scarf

It strayed about her head and neck like a
Rumour of something she had never done
Because, the moment ripe, she had no mind to
Yet might have done often, had she chosen.
Where in God's name, I wondered, does it begin
And where on earth may I imagine its end?
Indolent headlands smiled at me, labyrinthine
Rivers flowing into each other wound
And wound about her like desires to praise
Every movement that her body made.
As she moved, so did headlands, rivers too,
Shifting with her as the winter sun laid
Emphasis on colours rumoured in its rays,
Grey-flecked lines of white, delirium of blue.

The Lislaughtin Cross

*The Lislaughtin Cross is now in the National Museum in Dublin.
On the upper portion of the shaft and on the two arms of the front
there is a Black Letter inscription in Latin which in translation reads:
'Cornelius, son of John O'Connor, captain of his nation, and Juliana,
daughter of the Knight, caused me to be made by the hand of William,
son of Cornelius, June 4th, 1479.'*

William O'Connor was made when he made me
That others might adore
God of field and road, shore and river.

Some thought that I was made to be destroyed,
Burned the holy Abbey,
Murdered the calm men of God.

My rescuer ran until his terror and exhausted heart
Forced him to drop me
In the waiting earth of Ballymacassey

Where I lay three hundred years,
My golden body sinking
Deeper into the blackness,

A sun
Pitched into a dark
Waiting to cradle men,

A midnight not expecting morning,
The stillness of two hearts
Entered in each other.

A man named Jeffcott
Found me with his plough.
O see me now

Lifted from that lightless place
Where I understood the dead
And the blunderers above my head

Thumping to and fro
Building and breaking their worlds,
Bursting with get and go

Until they sank into the blackness where I lay,
Inviolate.
I stand now, polished in the light,

Saved from a repose
Impossible to speak of.
I lay so long at the heart of love

I am content to stand in this arranged place,
Upright, immaculate
Prisoner behind glass,

Hoarding in myself the touch of hands, of eyes,
The cries that cannot cease,
The black peace.

Book

You come to me with such avid eyes
I wonder what you expect to find.
When you turn my pages

It is not me you see, but you.
Is there anywhere in the world
You do not meet yourself?

What the rain writes on the ground is for you alone.
What the wind screams between the houses
Cannot so be heard by any other man.

You see and hear the wind and rain
And never know the pain
That made me.

Something has sentenced you to yourself.
Your only world is where you are,
What your eyes look at,

Open or shut.
You are an unspeakable secret,
A prison that walks about.

When you consider me
You involve me in your secret.
I extend and deepen it,

I enlarge you as I lose myself, word by word.
I am part of a story you invent
Like a rumour you once heard

And decided to make your own.
When you believe you possess me
You are most alone.

Lightning

At a decent distance
From the heads of men
I happen

And am gone.
This is how
I light up heaven

And define the dark.
You think I must
Be something of an exhibitionist,

A dramatic braggart of light?
I am a mere moment
Between this and that

Yet so much that moment
I
Illumine the sky

And the small homes of men,
Flash through their fears, spotlight their joys.
My deepest nature is quiet and private.
I cannot escape the noise.

Shell

I cannot say I came from nothing
But so it seemed when the sea
Began to shape me. How long

It took is not important.
Light and dark passed through me.
Nothing was constant

But the labouring
Fingers of the sea
At their grind of love and making.

This happened where few
Would wish to penetrate
And none could see

But I received my body there
And hid within me
All the voices of my maker

Singing of his work
As I lurched and tumbled
Through the unfathomed dark.

I bear, I am forever borne.
I am complete yet I must turn
And spin with the deep will, a form

Content to be
The still, perfect image of the sea
Or its demented plaything in a storm.

Sea

I am patient, repetitive, multi-voiced,
Yet few hear me
And fewer still trouble to understand

Why, for example, I caress
And hammer the land.
I do not brag of my depths

Or my currents, I do not
Boast of my moods or my colours
Or my breath in your thought.

In time I surrender my drowned,
My appetite speaks for itself,
I could swallow all you have found

And open for more,
My green tongues licking the shores
Of the world

Like starved beasts reaching for men
Who will not understand
When I rage and roar

When I bellow and threaten
I am obeying a law
Observing a discipline.

This is the rhythm
I live.
This is the reason I move

In hunger and skill
To give you the pick of my creatures.
This is why I am willing to kill,

Chill every created nerve.
You have made me a savage master
Because I know how to serve.

The Island

I

Consider the sea's insatiate lust
And my power of resistance.

The waves' appetite
Gives me reason to exist,

This undermining
This daily assault on my body

Keeps me singing
Like the larks that rise from my heather.

The sea would swallow me whole
But I am a shelter
For music that startles the sky.
In my fields and furrows
Is rhythm to rival the sea.

Is this why we fight?
Does my hidden music
Draw the sea to my throat

To suck my secrets into itself?
Must two kinds of music
Clash and devour
Till the crack of whatever doom lies in store?

I am always about to surrender
When the sea withdraws from my shore

And leaves me to hear my own music again.
Nothing stranger!
I am consoled
By the voices of creatures
Whose wings are made of my pain.

II

This morning my fields sigh with relief
Because they have survived a storm.
When the sea explodes in rage or grief

What can they do but take it as it comes?
My fields are not interested
In suicide or martyrdom

But in green joyful endurance,
In those changes that are mine also.
If I could imagine a happy man

He would be like my fields before
And after storm.
He would live close to the battered shore

But flourish in his own way.
He would accept the sky's changes
Absorb its fury

Be an image of repose in its light.
But I know nothing of men
And must content myself with

Green peace that knows how to survive.
Worse storms, I know, are gathering
But my fields will live.

Bread

Someone else cut off my head
In a golden field.
Now I am re-created

By her fingers. This
Moulding is more delicate
Than a first kiss,

More deliberate than her own
Rising up
And lying down.

I am fine
As anything in
This legendary garden

Yet I am nothing till
She runs her fingers through me
And shapes me with her skill.

The form that I shall bear
Grows round and white.
It seems I comfort her

Even as she slits my face
And stabs my chest.
Her feeling for perfection is

Absolute.
So I am glad to go through fire
And come out

Shaped like her dream.
In my way
I am all that can happen to men.
I came to life at her finger-ends.
I will go back into her again.

The Sandwoman

After the tide went out this morning
The islandboy started to make me out of sand.
How clear and purposeful he was, concentrating
On my head, neck, shoulders, breasts, hands,
All my body made from sand of the sea.
I heard the horizon whisper its awe
When the islandboy stood back and looked at me
Who'd been imagined according to his law.

Then, with the tide on the turn, he touched me
As he'd not touched me in the making.
He kissed my face and hands, he loved me then
As the sea returned to witness his ecstacy.
I swallowed his sheer seed, my body breaking
Where the raping waves dispersed me into grains again.

Silence

Once I was the heartbeat of the world
But am an outcast now.
Why do you find it so difficult

To live with me? I live behind
The eyes of men,
I am the brother of loneliness

And I have never betrayed my kind.
Myself is non-assertion,
A shadow on the ground,

Someone always in the wings
Or just outside the room
Where the party grows exciting,

Voices rising higher
As the night advances.
I do not ask that you should think of me

But of yourself
And what is in you.
I am in you

And wait for you to recognise me there.
Come towards me, I am all there is
Of mercy and repose

For those who drown
Into my deepest lake of sympathy.
I offer no more than

The secret of the dove's breast
On a branch at dawn,
The white fields of December

Purged of contradiction,
Whatever is ignored and gentle,
Your proper calm,

My old capacity
To listen and to trust.
I will be speechless when I wait for you
For when I speak, I'm lost.

May the Silence Break

Because you do not speak
I know the shock
Of water encountering a rock.

Supremacy of silence is what I hate.
Only gods and graves have a right to that
Or one who knows what this is all about.

Perhaps you do.
If so, let something break through
The walls of silence surrounding you.

Out here among words
Your silence is the magnet I am drawn towards.
Men's mouths, animals' eyes and the throats of birds

Fear this impenetrable thing.
So do I, all day long
And when the night drops like a confirmation

Of what you are,
Controller of every star,
Possessor

Of what the daylight struggled to reveal.
This possession kills
Whatever it wills.

Nothing I say matters tonight.
Nor should it.
This silence is right

Because it knows it is.
I shiver in the cocksure ice
And long for the warmth of bewildered eyes.

May the silence break
And melt into words that speak
Of pain and heartache

And the hurt that is hard to bear
In the world out here
Where love continues to fight with fear

And the war on silence will end in defeat
For every heart permitted to beat
In the air that hearts make sweet.

The Burning of Her Hair
(after Ovid)

I burst out in anger:
'For God's sake, don't silver-bleach your hair!'
No need for bleaching now. Your hair is gone.
Bald woman!
Imagine! You had incomparable hair
So silky-thrilling to the touch even girls' expert fingers
Baulked at braiding it, finer than the best
Silk of Asian girls at a feast,
Delicate as a spider's thread,
Its colours playing in a never-before-seen light.
Every time I looked, I saw it had
Changed, it was never the same sight
Twice, rippling, waving a hundred ways,
The comb's teeth never marked it, it was
Shy, bright, wild, it had never heard
The bruising anger of a human word,
Girls who dressed it had no fear, they knew
A love their blood confirmed was true,
No hairpin scratched their skin.

                              I have seen
You so at morning, naked, drowsily at rest
When young sunlight kissed your breasts,
Your hair a lazy, scattered magic on your shoulders,
Yourself a happy refugee from over beauty's border
Imprisoned in my stare
Your hair
All unaware
Innocent as first feathers

Surviving inquisitions, tribunals, terror, dread
Of heated irons pressing at your head.

'Don't burn it, don't torture it to death,' I said,
'Have mercy on your hair, gentle it, treat it well,
Don't force it into rings and waves of hell,
Let the wind tend it, the attentive wind, let the wind
Dress it so it claims all my heart and mind.
The wind is privileged to be
Responsible for this beauty.'

                             And now it's gone,
Charred, dirty, wronged, its light
The poisoned eyes of a broken-backed rat.
I saw a painting once, a goddess whose seawashed hair
Was almost yours.
You're stricken now, stupefied, appalled or
Simply not believing the mirror.
No jealous girl would run the risk
Of making you grotesque,
No scented queen of a beauty parlour
Reduce you to this horror.
Yourself! You only have yourself to blame!
Never mind! From conquered Germany will come
Hair to give you a new name.
When a man fixes on your false hair
You'll think 'This idiot loves a German stranger,
He doesn't even see me. A few days ago, I
Could have shown him hair to make him dizzy!'

                         I hear your small, burned cries.
I see the charred dribs and drabs stuck to your knees.
Your ruined head
Knows justice is dead.
But don't cry, my dear, stop, stop crying!
In no time at all your hair will be growing.
No burning could keep such glory down,
No torture guarantee its final destruction.
One day soon, every man in this hurrying town
Will stop and gape and stare
And say 'My God! What hair! What fantastically beautiful hair!'

We Are Living

What is this room
But the moments we have lived in it?
When all due has been paid
To gods of wood and stone
And recognition has been made
Of those who'll breathe here when we are gone
Does it not take its worth from us
Who made it because we were here?

Your words are the only furniture I can remember
Your body the book that told me most.
If this room has a ghost
It will be your laughter in the frank dark
Revealing the world as a room
Loved only for those moments when
We touched the purely human.

I could give water now to thirsty plants,
Dig up the floorboards, the foundation,
Study the worm's confidence,
Challenge his omnipotence
Because my blind eyes have seen through walls
That make safe prisons of the days.

We are living
In ceiling, floor and windows,
We are given to where we have been.
This white door will always open
On what our hands have touched,
Our eyes have seen.

A Greasy Pole

The life of any ghost is a search for peace.
See a woman laughing, a man making bread,
A soiled newspaper thrown on a chair
Waiting for a tired reader,
You have the life of the dead.

It is an old intensity made new
For you and me
On our way in a boat to Tarbert regatta,
A pillowfight on a greasy pole
Above a chuckling sea

Whose amusement spreads to Asia
Thrown like an old coat across the map
Of the world as though to keep it warm.
Listen to Lynch's yell vanishing into the water.
That's the style, they cry. That man is in form.

If he keeps this up, he'll make a fortune,
A name for himself, a choice of wives.
The years are salty drops on his freckled shoulders.
Above the spectatorial sea, the dead
Are fighting for their lives

And the boats are still arriving at the long
Grey-stoned quay
Discharging those who mingle
With the people shouting welcome on the shore,
Ghosts of you and me.

A Kind of Trust

I am happy now.
You rose from your sick bed
After three weeks. Your heart was low

When the world grew small,
A white ceiling
And four yellow walls.

Let me say again what this means
To me. As far as I know
Love always begins

Like a white morning
Of seagulls near the window,
Messengers bringing

Word that we must up and out
Into a small garden
Where there are late

Apples we shall find
So ripe that the slightest touch
Will pitch them to the ground.

Best things seem content to fall and fail.
I am not good enough for that.
I fight the drag and pull

Of any kind of dying
And bitterly insist
On that white morning

When you weakly climb the stairs,
Letting new life reach you like a gift
There at the brown bannister.

I do not insist
Out of panic or vague dread
But out of a kind of trust

In this beginning
With late apples and early seagulls
And a young sun shining

When you let cold water flow into a cup,
Steady yourself between two chairs
And stand straight up.

A Passionate and Gentle Voice

Whatever contact I have with hope
Is clear to me on certain mornings
When a voice slips

Into my mind like a shy
Suggestion of love
That nothing will deny.

It is a passionate and gentle voice
Authentic as a patch of sunlight
On a floor inside a window

And it has always spoken the same words:
'I live in the stripped branch,
Dying flowers on the kitchen table,

Pools of water after a storm
Uncomprehending as children
Strayed from their parents in a crowded town.

You understand I do not exhort.
My state is one of waiting
For you, for the most part,

And I am helpless till you observe me
With your electric blood
And your eyes

Redeemed from tedium by the desire
To know
Why something begins to stir

In utter stillness like a memory
That will not let you sleep at night
But takes possession of you

And absorbs you into itself.
So I await that morning
When you emerge

From the tired night as from a mist
Into a decision of sunlight
Where I exist.'

Separation

It breathes through the cherries,
Corn, virgin branches,
Hurts the eyes

Riveted on a dirtroad
Where stones snarl
At the car's backside

And a black squirrel electrifies an oak.
It walks in the wake of a forest fire,
Shells of trees hang like

A haggard army,
Roads without signs lead nowhere,
There are always some local gods wishing to

Lead us astray
Though we may be lost already.
With what gloomy defiance

It resists analysis
Though willing enough to reveal
Something in images –

Slow-motion pitch
And skid down the black face
Of a cliff,

Rainbow filth of oil
In a rut of water,
Dull

Seepage of self through grass
Seeking the ravenous kings
That set up their abode

In the dead and edible.
Oh yes
Many times it has come to this

But this, even this
(Heaven itself is but a glimpse)
Leads to the kiss

In the unknown village in the mountains,
Brings me the whitest knowledge
From the blood of shame

And asks salvation, the stranger, the reticent man
To open the door of his house
That I go in.

Willow

To understand
A little of how a shaken love
May be sustained

Consider
The giant stillness
Of a willow

After a storm.
This morning it is more than peaceful
But last night that great form

Was tossed and hit
By what seemed to me
A kind of cosmic hate,

An infernal desire
To harass and confuse,
Mangle and bewilder

Each leaf and limb
With every vicious
Stratagem

So that now I cannot grasp
The death of nightmare,
How it has passed away

Or changed to this
Stillness,
This clean peace

That seems unshakeable.
A branch beyond my reach says
'It is well

For me to feel
The transfiguring breath
Of evil

Because yesterday
The roots by which I live
Lodged in apathetic clay.

But for that fury
How should I be rid of the slow death?
How should I know

That what a storm can do
Is to terrify my roots
And make me new?

A Viable Odyssey

I sit by the fire
Watching flameworlds leap and vanish.
It happens again – the desire

For another world and so,
Encouraged by a modest winter sun,
I go

To look at the sea.
The sea does not seek the wind
Nor the wind the sea

Yet the wind
Makes the sea shiver and blush
Like a boy whose mind

Is touched by images that come
From somewhere outside
And will not leave him alone

Till he goes in search
Of what takes him
Past bank and brothel, theatre, church,

Where disappointment lies.
When I stand where the sea is crisp
I think the wind tries

To upset it, or find
The sea bristles and frowns
To accommodate the wind.

Suddenly the sky is ice.
I feel on my head
The grey threat burst

Till it hurts my bones.
Whatever I looked for
I forget at once

And run from the thing I found
As little spiteful hailstones
Hammer the helpless ground.

I draw few lessons from ice
Except the conviction
That in winter fire is

Better company. Kind flames greet
My searching body
Warming to defeat.

To You

I pass under the lamplight.
In that yellow world
I realise the night

Speaks its own language,
A dark idiom swelling
Perhaps with rage

Or love. I try to listen
But the words scurry
To the backs of stars. When

I tell myself I should settle for silence
Since better men have said
It is the purest eloquence

Leaves whisper at my feet
Or raise their rhetoric
About my head. What

Are my foolish words when
Set against the last gasp
Of a wave over a stone

Or the intense disclosures
Of shadows
Dancing together?

Nothing. Yet it is this
Nothing that compels me
To wake in the nightsilence

And feel the need to speak
To you. This is a universe
Of voices. They make

Me want to be a voice
Telling my fragments in words
That bid your heart rejoice

At the spider lunging to the kill,
Every sharp unshareable pain,
Dust that gathers on the window-sill.

The Furies

When the furies come
Their eyes stupid and bright
Hoofing into the room

How in God's name
May we hope
To cope with them

As they sit here,
Humped and dumb
Around the fire?

They do not respond to words
But take the shapes
Of starved carrion birds

Ready to feed
On reputation, love, kindness
Or hot bread.

Which they do
Until their own boredom moves them
To try something new

So they go together
Like a dull herd
In stupifying weather

And I realise
The mind's release in your words,
The heart's release in your eyes.

The Moment of Letlive

When you look at me askance
In a moment I become
All I know of tolerance,

Altruism born of pain.
Gouged out of life for the most part
It questions what I am of man

And hurts me into love.
I hold your agony in my hands
And feel it enter me as if

Self cannot be contained
Within the body.
I am stunned

By this pained flowing
Out of your blood
But I have known

The moment of letlive
When it seemed possible
To subdue the beast

That turned your days to fear
And crouched in the corner of the room
Sneering.

Beyond Knowledge

On this quiet afternoon
When the shadows of branches
Make trembling sculpture
On a cracked wall
And a gull's cries
Recall the eyes
Of dying children,
I know enough to know
Most things worth knowing
Are beyond knowledge.

And I have now
The most chilling sense
Of the ignorance
That keeps us all from
Leaping into the abyss.
Down there is revelation
Or oblivion. Perhaps
They are one and the same.
Up here, some live as though
They were kings of knowledge.
The most ridiculous figure of all is your
Expert.
The only expert is death,
A most ubiquitous fellow,
There's nobody he doesn't know
And to this end, is not above
Crashing the party
Like some barging junior executive
Randy for brandy.
As he seeks introductions all round, I see
There are worse things than walking
Knowing one's limited
Capacity for love,
Half-glimpsing the most
Terrifying images in the March grass
Or on the pavement of a cul-de-sac
Or in a small
Apparently uncared-for garden,

Feathers ripped from the body
Of a robin killed when
We were sleeping,
His eyes closed in final
Terror or disbelief,
Or in this room the sound
Of your voice in sleep, torn words, half-crying,
And towards morning the sense
Of a world withdrawing
From you, from me, from all
We seem to half-know.
I lie here and watch it go
Through the wise light.
It has been so patient with us
I wish to thank it
As I witness its retreat
But reach instead
Towards you, limp in sleep,
And touch your head.

Swanning

This pair of swans were perfect as you'd find
In any lake or river in the land
Till for reasons quite unknown to humankind
Hatred grew between them wickedly and
They parted, one to each end of the lake
Where they had lived in harmony for years,
White splendour sundered now for hatred's sake,
Dividing water making huge V's of fear

Between the stately two. Still as snow, they stared
Each other down the grey expanse,
Two lovers, it seemed, silently crying,
Unable to speak. Then they flew, breasts bared,
Beaks eager as knives. They clashed in fury once,
Twice, many times, thrashed, broke, lay there, dying.

Honey

That morning I might easily have passed by
The brown leaf, the green twig, the black stone,
But a frantic buzzing caught my ear and I
Stopped, looked all around, then up, then down.
On the grey pavement two bees were locked in
Each other's bodies like lovers gone mad.
Such ferocity was hardly known even
To man. By leaf, twig and stone they struggled

Stabbing with tiny knives, beating thin wings
Till one topped the other. Yet how strange –
It was the one beneath that stung his enemy dead.
The buzzing stopped. He crawled on top, dragging
His victim in unabatable rage,
Sucking honey from its body, blood from its head.

The Speech of Trees

The ceiling is lonely
The walls are lonely
The trees shiver with eloquence
Where have you gone?
There is a sound behind all sound
The sound of souls
Rustling each other like trees
In a clipping wind.
A friend died yesterday
A friend will die today
A child will be abandoned
A girl go to Libya
('There must be people somewhere who say what they think')
Where have you gone?
The speech of trees gives nothing away,
If I could listen truly
I might hear what they have to say

And find some reason
Why your speech is like the speech of trees.
I cannot listen.
Where have you gone?

Wish

Out of the matted tangle of lies
Out of my betrayal of you
Your betrayal of me
Out of the crossed sea and the Star of David
Out of the jokes in the dreary streets
Of the cities where we never knew each other
Out of every accursed boring moment
When hatred furnaced our faces
And we knew that love can happen only
Between strangers for a moment in a cold place
Then gutter and cease

Out of the floors the walls the ceilings
Of houses where we fumbled through each other
Like branches swaying touching parting touching
I wish you peace.

Knives

Love is a knife in the daylight.
I shift, shiver, stabbed by an old thought
Of her shining like a blade
At my side.

Loneliness is a knife. As I sit
And cut my heart into interesting pieces
I see you walking down a street,
A stranger's face defining strangers' faces.

Straying

His mouth festers in the kneeling garden,
He longs for my kiss, he climbs to his betrayal,
He is my wounded bull, he is divine and dull,
He is the green skirt of the woman I will never fuck,
He is the dog at her breast,
He is the theatre in the river
Where I laughed my guts up
He is the girl writing this for me
He is the lost parcel in the pub
He is the genuine heretic
He is my daughter
He is my secondhand book
He is the glad aching of my prick
He is the forgotten thing
The hated vespers
Knitting machine
Josie Mulvihill's eyes
The small pump outside Jack Enright's
The dirty lane leading to death

The milky way
The women without milk
The men without seed
Cotton wool, the blood of farmers,
The black cat responding to my call.
I am washing Debbie Sullivan's toes,
She is worried about the Propagation of the Faith.
Nobody here has ever spoken about pollution.
Jack Lynch is working in the mill.
He will die leaning over a five-barred gate.
There will be hard times but we'll mend them.
Sweet though women are they cannot reach a man.
This is the cluttered time, the eyes of boys at corners
Flicker like spiders where boys find it hard to climb
But they will, they will,
Outside the banked house where the half-blind woman
Is lusting for my father.
Eva! Eva! Her name is a bomb in the river,
Slut, bitch, cunt, saint, mother, daughter, whore.
There have been others. There will be more.
I nourish poison in my blood.
I am straying home to God.

Phone Call

A woman rings me at three in the morning to say
Fuck. Nothing else. Just fuck. Again fuck.
At that hour I'm not at my social
Best and don't know what to say back

To the voice. Yet I will not hang up.
I know the language of love and prayer,
I like that woman's voice and drowsily
Wonder what is the colour of her hair.

I hear
Womansadness pouring into my ear,
Sadness rivering heart and brain.

From Asia and Africa and India she speaks
On the phone at three in the morning to me.
Fuck. Sadness is never obscene. Fuck again.

Keep in Touch

Like the birdthroats
Of a winter's morning
Anticipating Spring

Flinging into our ears
Notes
We had almost forgotten

Or the ice we had begun
To accept as unbreakable
Melting in the sun

To resurrect the grass;
Like the neighbour
Who took ship one morning

Eleven years ago
To see a country
Where the snow

Lasts for nearly half the year
And then returned
As though from the next street

Where he had bought milk and bread,
Bringing stories that seemed like glad
Reports from the land of the dead –

Keep in touch, keep in touch,
My friend, my love.
When the old boredom begins to approach

With its ice in the blood,
Its manic wish
To shrivel and impoverish,

Keep in touch because I will be
Waiting for a word from you.
It means more to me

Than I can say
Or you imagine
That on any indistinguishable day

I touch through my hands, see through my eyes
Your face on the far side of the abyss
Bringing surprise.

Star

Does not complain
When gaped at,
Bother to reply when

Lied about,
Remains unmoved
When someone with his wits

On fire begins
To worship it as though
In expiation of his sins.

It sees starved hearts from where
It may become
A confirmation of their fear

Or the convenient food
Of busybodies
Ravenous for distant gods.

They turn on it
And curse its silence.
It will not blab or prate

In answer to each troubled whine
But is
Here, now, as it has been,

Will be,

Star in its own sky,
Fire of time,
White eye of eternity.

High Planes

Clouds that blot but don't obscure the sky
Always attract and sometimes
Mesmerise the eye

When high planes trail among them,
Seen but unheard.
Small, perfect gods

On the run
From adoration
Cherish their distance

Hard achieved.
Certain moments when
We have truly loved

Have had this height, this distance,
This mute momentum,
This reticence,

This moving away.
I cannot say
I see the high planes often

But when I do, I stand
Dumb with admiration.
Something that concerns me

Is taken out of my hands
And perfected
Way above my head

In a spectacular silence.
I have no need to worry
About the outcome of such journeys

Because what I briefly see
Is without flaw.
I cherish this brevity

And keep the high planes in my mind
When they've gone so far the sky
Reverberates without them, without a sound.

Proof

I would like all things to be free of me,
Never to murder the days with presupposition,
Never to feel they suffer the imposition
Of having to be this or that. How easy
It is to maim the moment
With expectation, to force it to define
Itself. Beyond all that I am, the sun
Scatters its light as though by accident.

The fox eats its own leg in the trap
To go free. As it limps through the grass
The earth itself appears to bleed.
When the morning light comes up
Who knows that suffering midnight was?
Proof is what I do not need.

Birth

I don't know if I shall be
Speaking or silent, laughing or crying,
When it comes to me

Out of its own distant place
To shine at the window, rustle the curtains,
Brush my face

More lightly than gossamer,
So inspiring and fragile
I shall not dare to stir

Or hardly breathe until I sense
In my heart and mind
Its delicate omnipotence.

I may know then
The price and value of stillness
Commonly ignored by men

And be content to feel
It possess me,
Steal

Through my remotest countries
And establish its rule
Where, my bravest days,

I would not dare to venture.
Then, if I find courage enough,
I may speak in a manner

Befitting this thing.
God help me the moment
My heart starts opening

To comprehend and give.
I will be born in that hour of grace.
I will begin to live.

Let It Go

Let it go
Out of reach, out of sight,
Out of the door and the window,

Through the city,
Over the mountains
And the sea.

I do not mean a mere escape,
A deliberate loosening
Of a brutal grip

Like that of church on soul,
Father on son
Or even love on the lover's beautiful

Surrender to the dear pain,
Or any sin or sickness that could
Swallow a man.

I mean a different thing
Beyond desire to acquire or captivate,
A felt relinquishing

Such as can be seen
When the air yields to the bird
Or the green

Trunk of a tree surrenders
To the tactful advance of moss
Or when the river stirs

Its surface
To accept a drifting stick.
I feel such courtesy

When I let it go
From me to countries
I will never know

And I stand, hoping to discern
Its breath in my heart
At its return.

The Whiteness

No dream that I remember
Can touch it.
Not even my childspicture of Christ's cloak

On Easter morning was white as this.
It surpassed
The white bounce of the waterfall

And the secret of wheat.
It put to shame
The names of girls

And the frosty breath of old men,
Fingers of women who have lost blood
In their sickness

And seem hardly able to contain
Heaven
Bursting through their skin.

It was whiter than the whitest part of my mind
Or a sheet of paper lying on the table
Undefiled by words.

Though I could not look at it
It enveloped me.
I drowned in the whiteness,

Felt it filtering through every gross bone,
Cold and impeccable.
I was in a country where sin was unknown

And error did not exist.
It was simply that because of the whiteness
Ice and rain and mist

Could not be thought of.
In the whiteness there seemed no need
Even of love.

Which, I believe, was why
I closed my eyes to find the darkness,
To try to banish the whiteness.

And I did.
And I found
A scatter of ants on the ground

And though they blundered hither and thither
Like drunken guests at a wedding
They did not maul each other

But did what they had to do at my feet
Before my eyes
From which the whiteness is vanishing still
Though it never dies.

A Giving

Here in this room, this December day,
Listening to the year die on the warfields
And in the voices of children
Who laugh in the indecisive light
At the throes that but rehearse their own
I take the mystery of giving in my hands
And pass it on to you.

I give thanks
To the giver of images,
The reticent god who goes about his work
Determined to hold on to nothing.
Embarrassed at the prospect of possession
He distributes leaves to the wind
And lets them pitch and leap like boys
Capering out of their skin.
Pictures are thrown behind hedges,
Poems skitter backwards over cliffs,
There is a loaf of bread on Derek's threshold
And we will never know who put it there.

For such things
And bearing in mind
The midnight hurt, the shot bride,
The famine in the heart,
The demented soldier, the terrified cities
Rising out of their own rubble,

I give thanks.

I listen to the sound of doors
Opening and closing in the street.
They are like the heartbeats of this creator
Who gives everything away.
I do not understand
Such constant evacuation of the heart,
Such striving towards emptiness.

Thinking, however, of the intrepid skeleton,
The feared definition,
I grasp a little of the giving
And hold it close as my own flesh.

It is this little
That I give to you.
And now I want to walk out and witness
The shadow of some ungraspable sweetness
Passing over the measureless squalor of man
Like a child's hand over my own face
Or the exodus of swallows across the land

And I know it does not matter
That I do not understand.

Sacrifice

How it was lived through her –
This giving of herself
That she never understood,

A sacrifice
A customary selflessness
A decimation and scattering of herself

To the four winds of the insatiate future.
Whatever men and women waited there
Were unknown to her

As the rain's lisping or belting secrets
At her windows
In the sleepless time.

And to what end?
To let some perfection steal through
Barely distinguishable days and nights of her life?

A device that helped her
Never to see herself?
A wish to imprint some version of herself

On the self of the unknown?
She listened to the rain,
To the rowdy wind,

To the gabble of unseen birds,
To the words of those under
What she took to be her care,

And felt something like love
Bleeding from her,
Wounding, renewing, confusing,

Like the touch of her fingers on another's skin,
The contact and vacancy
Of the aftermath of pain.

The Fire is Crying

There are nine sods of turf in the fire,
Three at the centre flawlessly stacked,
Humpy brown ones on either side,
Black towers at the back,
It is a desert, a forest, a city,
Architecture of my own
Emptiness blazing under an exiled sky.

For the first time in my life as a man
I see a woman's face in the fire,
A long face, serious. Her hair is black,
Her skin grief-lined. She has the look
That knows the flesh is falling from her.

The hair tumbles to one side, the lips shake,
The fire is crying for her breaking neck.

A Half-Finished Garden

Because her days were making a garden
She haunted that particular beach
Drawing rocks, sticks, shells and stones,
Random-pitched sea-gifts, over the years.
Bog-oak, sculpted and twisted,
She lugged from the beach up to the garden
That was half-finished when she had to leave it
To go to a place of which I know nothing.

Here is the picture (I have nothing but pictures),
The sea helpless to govern its giving
Through rumble and slither, bang, roar and hiss,
A house on a cliff-top with staring blue windows
And, work of the dead to pleasure the living,
A half-finished garden, epitaph, promise.

Her Face

The scrupulous and piercing hand of love
Wrote a few true lines into her face
Along the forehead, cheeks, about the eyes.
Her face was kind, or kind enough
To those who looked in it for hope or help
As if it were a holy well where men
And women came to stare into themselves,
To find the loving stranger buried deep within.

Her face drank pain, still offered its slow smile
As though the days were hungry and cried for bread,
As though itself, being lost, itself could save.
Her face sickened, either temple was a hole
Deep enough to contain the world's dead.
Her face broke in the grave, and is the grave.
O she is rich if she receives
The barest shred of what she gave.

A Restoration

Was it the lazy haze of the summer afternoon
Drifting into her, or the warm
Indolence of the sea caressing every bone
That made her stretch out on the sandy grass
And give herself into the arms
Of this prolonged, seductive moment?
Was she free a while of children's cries
Boring through her, shrill and insistent?
Whatever it was, she suddenly knew she was naked
And glancing at her left hand
Saw her marriage ring was missing.
She was panic as she searched and searched
Until she found it in the thieving ground
And restored it to its mark, dark and shining.

She Sees Her Own Distance

Let no black disasters stop her course
When she, in the exploding countryside
Where boys like burning tyres are flung
High into fields and meadows to bleed

Into the all-receiving earth, decides
To let her daughter live in the world
Grinning on cynical axis. She knows this well
And yet she gives the child over to herself

To become what she is capable of becoming
Despite hurt speech, distressed hands, hungering eyes,
Despite do-gooders and civilised neglect.

She wishes the child well, waking, sleeping and dreaming.
Then, because she is suffering and wise,
She sees her own distance, and is not shocked.

More Dust

Love is nothing but the wish to love.
When I pitched the eel back over my head
And saw its wet wriggling in the dust
I ran from the river up to the road
Where a man was sweeping more dust
Into a barrow old as himself.
He was muttering about work and no rest
For the wicked, smiling. A small sweat
Chilled my back as I came to the door
And ran into the room.
                                    She stood
In front of the fire though it was summer.
I said nothing but ran up to her,
Laid my head against her belly.
I tried to listen to my brother.

Wings

The words have been said.
He towers above her, she pretends he's not there,
She concentrates on washing a heart of lettuce,
Wet leaves glitter in her fingers.
He folds his hand like wings about her black hair
And kisses her head.

A Music

It is not a music that will live alone
Or be acquired
For good by any man.

It was taken from the crest of a green wave
By a man among rocks
Who thought it sweet enough to beat the grave

And shaped it to the heartbeat that he knew.
It strayed through silent years
Mute as a swallow in the blue

Arena of summer, a flash
Of wing and breast
Less tangible, it seemed, than any childish wish.

I found it in a park in the city
And waited for it.
It came to me with a light dignity,

I took it, soon it was gone.
What I have now I do not own.
It is not a music that will live alone.

The Habit of Redemption

I have felt the world shrivel to days
Beckoning me
Into a hell of indifference

Until I found
The habit of redemption
Living in my mind.

It breathed in the morning
As I wrote a letter
To a woman in mourning

For her dead brother.
He was sixty-six
And rare,

His days touched by imagination.
He died in October
Tending his garden.

It reached the deepest part of me
When the middle-aged man
Raking leaves turned quickly

And said 'how are you?'
Autumn died at his feet
But the day was new.

I would say nothing about all this,
Never bother to mention
The moment's metamorphosis

Were it not that hell gapes
At every step.
What I am given is not a means of escape

But of confrontation,
The truest education
That I know.

Moment that is all moments
Be with me when I grasp
A little of the meaning of transience,

A hint of the infernal night.
Come in the shape of a blade of grass
Stuck to the side of my boot

Or a kind word from stranger or friend
Or a yellow shedding from an old tree
That will not bend.

A Glimpse of Starlings

I expect him any minute now although
He's dead. I know he has been talking
All night to his own dead and now
In the first heart-breaking light of morning
He is struggling into his clothes,
Sipping a cup of tea, fingering a bit of bread,
Eating a small photograph with his eyes.
The questions bang and rattle in his head
Like doors and cannisters the night of a storm.
He doesn't know why his days finished like this
Daylight is as hard to swallow as food
Love is a crumb all of him hungers for.
I can hear the drag of his feet on the concrete path
The close explosion of his smoker's cough
The slow turn of the Yale key in the lock
The door opening to let him in
To what looks like release from what feels like pain
And over his shoulder a glimpse of starlings
Suddenly lifted over field, road and river
Like a fist of black dust pitched in the wind.

A Winter Rose

Happy to speak of intertwining briars
Mingling to breed, let's say, a winter rose
More defiantly beautiful the fouler the weather
Till the world knows what its true nature is
But all I see is an old man standing there
His mind blasted, snot and tears in his face,
His fingers freezing into a shape like prayer,
His words falling to earth the feel of ice –
'God rest you, love! God love you, darling dear!'
Fingers unlock, lips shut, he turns from the grave,
Stumbles on other graves, small grassy hills,

He'll come tomorrow, speak, and will she hear?
He'll come, and come, although his mind must rave
To know she's dead, and time is what he kills.

The Names of the Dead Are Lightning

'All my old friends are dying,'
You say in your letter.
Last night the wind cried

Through the house and the rain
Flailed at the streets and trees.
I thought of your loss

Knowing too well,
If I tried for weeks,
Not a syllable

Would salve your wound.
Tice. Joe. Jackie. Gone.
Father, why does the sound

Of thunder make me seek
The darkest room in the house,
Sit and wait for the blue flick

Of lightning over the walls?
You know how I hate loud voices
But this voice called

As though it would not be denied
From heaven to earth, from earth
To heaven. All night I tried

To decipher its tone of cosmic command
But all I found was your letter
Flickering in my mind

The darkest place I know.
The names of the dead are lightning.
Tice. Jackie. Joe.

I See You Dancing, Father

No sooner downstairs after the night's rest
And in the door
Than you started to dance a step
In the middle of the kitchen floor.

And as you danced
You whistled.
You made your own music
Always in tune with yourself.

Well, nearly always, anyway.
You're buried now
In Lislaughtin Abbey
And whenever I think of you

I go back beyond the old man
Mind and body broken
To find the unbroken man.
It is the moment before the dance begins,

Your lips are enjoying themselves
Whistling an air.
Whatever happens or cannot happen
In the time I have to spare
I see you dancing, father.

The Third Force

The third force grows
Between a man and a woman
When their lives mingle more deeply
Than either knows.

They give to each other what they can give.
Beyond that, it seems they live
Giving everything else to the air
Where the third force grows in silent power
Saying Now it is time to cry
And Now it is time to know
Or to try to begin to know
Every consoling illusion
And what underlies conversation
Of rain whipping the night
And the damp pain in the bones
In rooms where others lived
Their given number of days
In their own forgotten ways.

When the third force decides to laugh,
To spread its particular light,
A man and a woman are happy
Delighting in late-night talk
Alone in the smiling dark
Beyond the world of work
Lurking round morning's corner,
An old wolf without teeth,
All impotence and threat.
The third force lives out its moods
In hearts that would reach each other
Affirming or mocking in one
Love or hate for the other,
Forever sure of itself,
Forever getting stronger,
Eating and drinking the feeling
That knots a man and a woman
In ways we all call human,
Each life a definition
Of the most engrossing loneliness,
Lucid within limits,
At home in the sense of loss,

Ignorant, rhythmical, blind
As this verse.
A man and a woman go their ways
Through streets and rooms of blame and praise
Among the blessingcurse.

Gestures

She passed me on the street
Her hand a quick white arc
Motioning brown hair –
Sweet Narcissus vanished in the crowd.

A girl that I knew better
Her mouth twisted in rage
Closed her eyes of a sudden
And stared at her own darkness.

One I love
Walked on a summer strand,
Bent and picked a shell,
Remarked on its intricacy,
Its scrupulous profundity,
Then tossed it into the sea.

Myself when young
Crouched near a rough mud wall
Seeking a sheltering shade
And covered my face with my hands.
Afraid.

Only gestures remain
To tell me the truth of things,
To grasp the flashing essences
That leap, scatter and die;
Only simple gestures
Confound the usual lie.

Westland Row

Brown bag bulging with fading nothings;
A ticket for three pounds one and six
To Euston, London via Holyhead:

Young faces limp, misunderstanding
What the first gay promptings meant –
A pass into a brilliant wilderness,
A Capital of hopeless promise.
Well, mount the steps: lug the bag:
Take your place. And out of all the crowd,
Watch the girl in the wrinkled coat,
    Her face half-grey.
    Her first time.

The Celtic Twilight

Now in the Celtic twilight, decrepit whores
Prowl warily along the Grand Canal
In whose rank waters bloated corpses float,
A dog and cat that came to a bad end.
The whores don't notice; perfumed bargainers
Prepare to prey on men prepared to prey
On them and others. Hot scavengers
Are victims, though they confidently strut
And wait for Dublin's Casanovas to appear –
Poor furtive bastards with the goods in hand.

And in the twilight now, a shrill whore shrieks
At one stiff client who's cheated her,
'Misther! If you come back again,
You'll get a shaggin' steel comb through the chest.'
Then gathering what's left of dignity,
Preparing once again to cast an eye
On passing prospects, she strolls beside
The dark infested waters where
Inflated carcases
Go floating by into the night
Of lurid women and predatory men
Who must inflict but cannot share
Each other's pain.

Moments When the Light

There are moments when the light
Makes me start up, fright
In my heart as if I feared to see
Unbearable clarity about me.
Once, on Portobello Bridge,
I had the sudden privilege
Of seeing light leap from the sky
About five o'clock on an autumn day,
Defining every visible thing,
Unseen by one among the moving throng;
Road, bridge, factory, canal,
Stained swans and filthy reeds, all
The set homegoing faces
Filling motorcars and buses;
Then I knew that energy is but
Unconsciousness; if moving men could
See where they are going, they would
Stop and contemplate the light
And never move again until
They understood why it should spill
A sudden benediction on
The head of every homegoing man.
But no one looked or saw the way
The waters danced for the visiting light
Or how green foliage glittered. It
Was ignored completely.
I knew the world is most at ease
With acceptable insanities,
Important nothings that command
The heart and mind of busy men
Who, had they seen it, might have praised
The light on Portobello Bridge.
But then, light broke. I looked. An evening glow.
Men go home because they do not know.

Ambulance

Shrieking on its mercy mission,
The white hysterical bully
Blows all things out of its way,
Cutting through the slack city
Like a knife through flesh.
People respect potential saviours
And immediately step aside,
Watching it pitch and scream ahead,
Ignoring the lights, breaking the rules,
Lurching on the crazy line
Between the living and the dead.

Hunchback

Day after twisted day, I carry it on
My back – this devil's hump, this mound
Of misery sprung from the roots in
My body's clay, grotesque companion
Of my wildest dreams. I have to bend
Beneath it, flame and rage
Because distortion is my closest friend,
The faithful ally of my youth and age.

Along the quays I walk and watch
The seagulls climbing in their flight
Or skimming the slow Liffey. Such
Perfection hurts my blood. In broad daylight,
My ugliness gapes like a wound while I,
Hands rammed in empty pockets, see
White miracles of grace on every side.
They circle to astonish and torment me.

Torment eats my heart. I see small ships
From Hamburg, Copenhagen. A sailor
Gamecocks on an upper deck. My lips
Form silently the names – Regina,
Honor Belle. Ships are women, queens
That ride the ocean, plough the sea,
Leaving the white foam of unrest where they have been,
Hacking hard voyages from port to port in me.

The outside world explores me but I
Am unknown territory, a secret river
Of obscure source, uncertain estuary.
I flow through time that time may yet deliver
Me from myself, my sense of well-made
Manhood from monstrous flesh and bone.
Creation preens itself, neat planets are displayed,
Jupiter wheels above me. I move alone.

The Liberties, Townsend Street, Stephen's Green,
Stations in my shuffling odyssey
Of old, appalling loneliness and pain;
While girls grow up and boys put out to sea
And women shape new histories in the womb,
I walk the streets of failure day and night,
Watching the symmetries life must assume,
Easy ships at anchor, able birds in flight.

O shapely world that I'm compelled to see
But be no part of, I move
Through your designs deliberately.
I feel a certain love
For what I see but cannot linger on;
Wet pavements shine at night, clean church-bells ring,
I stand where multitudes have come and gone –
The parody best proves the real thing.

Dublin: A Portrait

There the herds of eloquent phonies,
Dark realities kept in the dark,
Squalor stinking at many a corner
Poverty showing an iron hand;
There the tinker sprawls on the pavement,
Servile victim of those whose pence
He begs like a dog, his practised whining
For coins of pity making no sense.
There the gibbering lunatic wanders
Madly gesturing to the air,
Smiled at quietly by sane and simple,
His case unheard, his horror unshared.
Out in the suburbs the dead men prosper,
Spewed from the city at five o'clock,
Apathy snores in the telly jungle
Where corpses savour the rewards of work.
There the defeated gabbles his story,
Porter-sodden on a shaky stool,
Makes a drunken myth of deprivation,
Slashes the genuine, exalts the fool,
Mangles what passes his understanding,
Insists he knows genius to the bone,
Spitting assassin of whatever's worthy
Sets mediocrity on the throne.
Garrulous gossips hint and wrangle
In pub and parlour and seething street,
Rumours of rumours flash malignant
As Liffey slime in the cramped daylight.
Bulging churches tower in the greyness
Blocking out the light of the sun,
Holy frauds at their adoration
Bargain with God that they may get on:
Out in the darkness the sea is heaving
Corroding the shore in its roaring stealth,
Washing the feet of the stricken city,
Trying to purge its human filth.

Clearing a Space

A man should clear a space for himself
Like Dublin city on a Sunday morning
About six o'clock.
Dublin and myself are rid of our traffic then
And I'm walking.

Houses are solitary and dignified
Streets are adventures
Twisting in and out and up and down my mind.
The river is talking to itself
And doesn't care if I eavesdrop.

No longer cluttered with purpose
The city turns to the mountains
And takes time to listen to the sea.
I witness all three communing in silence
Under a relaxed sky.

Bridges look aloof and protective.
The gates of the parks are closed
Green places must have their privacy too.
Office-blocks are empty, important and a bit
Pathetic, if they admitted it!

The small hills in this city are truly surprising
When they emerge in that early morning light.
Nobody has ever walked on them,
They are waiting for the first explorers
To straggle in from the needy north

And squat down here this minute
In weary legions
Between the cathedral and the river.
At the gates of conquest, they might enjoy a deep
Uninterrupted sleep.

To have been used so much, and without mercy,
And still to be capable of rediscovering
In itself the old nakedness
Is what makes a friend of the city
When sleep has failed.

I make through that nakedness to stumble on my own,
Surprised to find a city is so like a man.
Statues and monuments check me out as I pass
Clearing a space for myself the best I can,
One Sunday morning, in the original sun, in Dublin.

A Visit

No.10 bus to the Park.
The conductor gives his promised shout.
I enter the house of the mad.

A late March day. The sun
Warms my back as I go in.
They sit, stand, walk, stare. Are alone.

No sharing this loneliness.
Unrelatedness
Is the skin on every face.

Unrelatedness.
I'd like to smash through this,
But find only an abyss. An abyss.

I've come to see a man.
I find him in the garden.
Flowers flourish all about him

But he is withering now,
Failing away from me.
I am stupid, cut off. How

Can I suggest a link?
I can neither speak nor think.
He speaks though, his eyes sunk

In his head.
Something about dolls he has made.
All around, the unreachable mad.

He has painted pictures too.
They cover the walls of his room.
Maybe I should see them sometime?

Yes I would. What are they about?
He can't say that.
I'll find out.

So.
After silence, I must go.
What else can I do?

As if I'd never been he sits there.
Mad flowers bloom everywhere.
Men and women stare at me. They stare.

Light Dying
In Memoriam Frank O'Connor (Michael O'Donovan)

Climbing the last steps to your house, I knew
That I would find you in your chair,
Watching the light die along the canal,
Recalling the glad creators, all
Who'd played a part in the miracle;
A silver-haired remembering king, superb there
In dying light, all ghosts being at your beck and call,
You made them speak as only you could do

Of generosity or loneliness or love
Because, you said, all men are voices, heard
In the pure air of the imagination.

126

I hear you now, your rich voice deep and kind,
Rescuing a poem from time, bringing to mind
Lost centuries with a summoning word,
Lavishing on us who need much more of
What you gave, glimpses of heroic vision.

So you were angry at the pulling down
Of what recalled a finer age; you tried
To show how certain things destroyed, ignored,
Neglected was a crime against the past,
Impoverished the present. Some midland town
Attracted you, you stood in the waste
Places of an old church and, profoundly stirred,
Pondered how you could save what time had sorely tried,

Or else you cried in rage against the force
That would reduce to barren silence all
Who would articulate dark Ireland's soul;
You knew the evil of the pious curse,
The hearts that make God pitifully small
Until He seems the God of little fear
And not the God that you desired at all;
And yet you had the heart to do and dare.

I see you standing at your window,
Lifting a glass, watching the dying light
Along the quiet canal bank come and go
Until the time has come to say good-night:
You see me to the door; you lift a hand
Half-shyly, awkwardly, while I remark
Your soul's fine courtesy, my friend, and
Walk outside, alone, suddenly in the dark.

But in the dark or no, I realise
Your life's transcendent dignity,
A thing more wonderful than April skies
Emerging in compelling majesty,
Leaving mad March behind and making bloom
Each flower outstripping every weed and thorn;
Life rises from the crowded clay of doom,
Light dying promises the light re-born.

Good Souls, to Survive

Things inside things endure
Longer than things exposed;
We see because we are blind
And should not be surprised to find
We survive because we're enclosed.

If merit is measured at all,
Vulnerability is the measure;
The little desire protection
With something approaching passion,
Will not be injured, cannot face error.

So the bird in astonishing flight
Chokes on the stricken blood,
The bull in the dust is one
With surrendered flesh and bone,
Naked on chill wood.

The real is rightly intolerable,
Its countenance stark and abrupt,
Good souls, to survive, select
Their symbols from among the elect –
Articulate, suave, corrupt.

But from corruption comes the deep
Desire to plunge to the true;
To dare is to redeem the blood,
Discover the buried good,
Be vulnerably new.

The Sin

Francis Xavier Skinner committed a sin.

It was a big sin, he thought,
A whopper,
An Everest of error,
A mortaller, as the man said,
Thinking of the price he'd have to pay when dead.

Skinner said to himself,
By this sin
I have wounded an innocent God.
I, Francis Xavier Skinner, have offended
The God of love.
That same God
Made everything that has been made.
But I have wounded him.

Skinner, a philosophical chap,
Considered it fit
To congratulate himself
On this extraordinary feat.
I cannot impress my friends, he thought,
But I can wound the God of love.
There's power for you!

And then he wondered,
What has happened to my sin?
Where has my big sin vanished?
Where have all the sins of the world vanished?
Is there a place where they go to hide?
Where does a fugitive sin reside?
Somewhere in hell perhaps
There's a sin-hospital
Where all the sins go to recover
From their conflict with God.
Do sins get bored and tired?
Do they play scrabble, ludo, draughts or dominoes?
Do they like to lie on the ground like winos
Outside a church on a Sunday morning
Begging pennies from respectable ladies

Whose souls are wrapped in their coats
Like mackerel in newspaper, their dead eyes
Old coins in the light, yesterday's news
Garbled in their skin,
Earthquakes shuddering in dandruff?
And then, having rested, do the sins get to their feet,
Amble off into the heart of some poor human
Who'll commit them all over again, as though for the first time,

Adam how-are-you?
And if one sin hurts God
What does he feel like after a million?
In a pretty bad way, I'd imagine,
Licking his wounds
Stretched on the floor of heaven,
Wondering
Is there any end to this damned repetition?
My divine arse is bored
By men who have murdered and lied
And thieved and deceived and whored
Ad nauseam.
I am bored. Therefore, I am.
O for a sin
Original
New
A sin
That will make my heart leap up to itself
My head spin
Down to you
Until I stand in the morning
Of my first creative excitement
On this dear dung-heap of a world
Calling
Cock-a-Doodle-Do.

Thoughtful soul that he was, Skinner wondered
What did that old excited God
Feel like
After my sin.
That shook him, I bet.
That gave him something to think about.

Did it really,
Did my sin hurt
The maker of the grass and the sea
The giver of my every heartbeat
The sweet creator of light
The image-maker in the dark
The fountain of grace and of truth
The first call of the cock in the morning
The last cry of my frightened mind?
Did my sin really hurt
Him?

Now that I think of it
I suspect my creator
May well be amused
By my sin.
Skinner, old son, you're a laughing-stock.
God smiles in the pleasant morning
Frowns in the storm
And if he ever noticed my sin
He was probably touched by its
Smallness, like a little bitchy insult
In a lost conversation.

I wonder, mused Skinner, is it possible
To be anything other than trivial?
Did I create Hell
To flatter my vanity?
How could any sin of mine
Be worthy of that Hell?
Hell is viciously divine!
Hell has such high standards
Though it is a low dive
Where all the unsaveable baddies
Get roasted alive.
Is all
My sinning
My own refusal to know
I am small?
Is there a sin
That God respects?

He must have respected Adam,
He threw him out of the garden,
But I won't imitate Adam.
When a sin is original
Imitation is fatal.
Mortal man is a spit in the wind.
Who cares how mortally he has sinned?

My trouble, said Skinner, is
I'm quite incapable of sin
On an honestly damnable scale.
I'm just another dwarfish vain male,
A puny son-of-a-bitch,
A spiritually juvenile offender.
I'll pray to my maker
To give me the vision
To commit a significant sin.

Dear God,
Give me the grace
To be a true sinner.

I'll be grateful forever.

Yours sincerely in Christ,

          Francis Xavier Skinner.

Six of One

1 *The Barbarian*

Applause he craves, music he loves, plus conversation
Plus working lunches plus the idea of progress
To which his days are a studied contribution.
The damned are a vulgar lot and he'll not bless
Them with enlightenment though there are some
To whom he'll show his sweetest disposition,
Even invite into his mind's kingdom
Where wisdom like a golden brooch is seen
Mesmeric as the thought of his own origin.
To accept one's true function is the problem.
Instruct the ignorant; ignorance is a sin.
Civilisation being the urge towards self-control
He makes articulate the pitifully dumb,
Dark souls lit with the glow of his own soul.

2 *The Expert*

The area is limited, it is true.
His knowledge of the area is not.
Right from the start, he knew what to do
And how to do it. All the fish he caught
Were salmon of knowledge and not once
Did he burn his thumb although he touched the fire
Of minds zealous as his own. God's a dunce
When the expert pronounces in his sphere
For he has scoured the fecund libraries
Till each one yielded all its special riches.
Prometheus, overworked and undersexed,
Files in his mind the succulent clarities
Knowing, from the ways of pricks and bitches,
Living is a footnote to the authentic text.

3   The Warriors

First, the leprechaun, gritty and sincere
Although his fairy rhetoric might spill
Like heaven upon all heads staring here
Till they felt clonked by some cosmic bible;
And then yon moon-faced fat above the beard
Blowing its dust across the helpless stones
Splutters to be heard, and will be heard
By all who see these two as paragons,
Warriors furring from the visionary north
To execute their comprehensive plan,
Improve the shabby towns, re-write the laws,
Assert for good their quintessential worth
Thus re-discovering heroic man
Pregnant with honour in service to The Cause.

4   The Missionary

Dear Souls, I am here on behalf of God.
My mind is made of His light.
I'm ready to shred my flesh, shed my blood
Doing His work among you. It
Is clear that all your gods must go
Back into the darkness from which they came.
I tell you this because I know.
You, your women and children will know the same.
Pray, O my brothers, for humility
And courage to surrender to the true.
Each man is a star, his soul is bright
As anything the heavens have to show.
Heaven's brightness flows to you from me
And on behalf of God I say, that's right.

5 The Convert

Reason, king of reasons, reigned alone.
There could never be another
Pretender to the throne
Of understanding. Mary, God's mother,
And other sweet begetters of the divine,
Together with all antics of the magic dark
Within the heart, were unquestionably fine
Illusions, especially when seen to work
For simple mortals. And then, one day,
In the broad sun, reason upped and slipped away
Restless, perhaps, for different air and food.
Our reasonable man felt quite distrait
And shocked admiring friends who heard him say
(He meant it too) 'Thank God! Thank God!'

6 The Savage Ego Is a Circus Tent

The savage ego is a circus tent
Containing the beasties and the people
Clapped together into a violent
Belch in the middle of a field.
Innocent eyes, as ever, widen at the sight
Of brave man swallowing fire;
Daddy is a surge of lost delight
Finding that tigers are what tigers were.
Elephants, snakes, the man on stilts,
Clowns, Fat Woman, mountain of happy lard,
Vivid fliers defying sternest laws
Replace the solid world that melts
Until no heart can ever again grow hard
Nor anything be heard except applause.

Lear in Africa

I killed the fool at the back of a grotty café
Half-way between the Arts and Science Buildings
Because I wouldn't let him goad me into saying
What remains for me to say. I hired a boy

To break into these white European-style houses,
Rob trivia, frighten the women, escape on foot
Through traffic. If he gets caught I hope they kill him too.
I caused a flood last night. You drowned in it

As did my daughter who is all my daughters, an intrepid girl
Though delirious, being no man's property but mine.
She must kill to survive while I survive to kill.
Such pithy jewels adorn the laws my armies call divine.

There is one chapter which causes me some trouble.
This is the source not of my raving but of my stammering.
To begin to think of it is to begin to cry like a fool.
I hate my endless tears; they force me to sing

Of being nothing, having nothing, coveting nothing
In a world of nothing, though spiders, vipers, bees
And underground, submarine strugglers/predators might stir me
To music which you might choose to interpret as praise.

If I sat here with you and saw your tears
I would sip them until they became my own.
O Africa! My last black chalice of agony
I will swallow you down

And cry through these glasses I have grown fond of
And cripple with insult whoever claps me on the back
And dedicate my increasing youth to stirring up trouble
And laugh at all thoughts caged in a book

Opening its maw for some disciplined, ravenous, tired mind to
        wander in
Looking for light, poor light, to see itself, the world, to see
The boy mangled in traffic, matchbox houses in the flood
Becoming débris in fields and roadsides, becoming me

Seeing you, young woman escaping with her sons
While old hands might happily murder you here.
For the tenth time tonight I wipe my trusty glasses
And see another Africa form in the shape of another tear.

O all my Africas
I are Lear
Dying to live
As though they / you / I
Were not parentchildren of fear.

The Pig

You, Heavenly Muse, how will you justify
The pig's ways to men?
How will you sing
Of the pig's origin?
What thighs opened wide
To let out that snout
Rammed on a carcase of timeless slime?
When the old sly juices went to work
What womb
Sheltered our little darling?
What breasts
Gave it suck?

Suck, suck.

And on our treacherous planet
What hearts worry for its welfare?

The pig is everywhere.

He grunts between the lovers in their bed
His hot sperm flooding the girl
His dungeon breath rutting into her skin
Where a man's fingers move in what he thinks

Are patterns of enchantment.
The pig's eyes smile in the dark.

The pig's eyes glow with ambition.
He knows that where his head won't go
His tail will enter,
His little corkscrew tail.

The pig sits on committees,
Hums and haws, grunts yes and no,
Is patient, wise, attentive,
Wary of decision (alternatives are many).
When he hefts his bottom from the chair
The seat is hot.
His head is dull
But, maybe, he's just a little stronger now.

The pig knows how to apologise.
He would hurt nobody.
If he did, he didn't mean it.
His small eyes redden with conviction.
Remorse falls like saliva from his jaws.

The pig is bored
But doesn't know it.
The pig gobbles time
And loves the weekend.
The pig is important
And always says 'It seems to me' and 'Yes, let's face it'.
The pig chews borrowed words,
Munching conscientiously.
Sometimes he thinks he's a prophet, a seer so elegant
That we should bow before him.
He is more remote from a sense of the unutterable
Than any words could begin to suggest.

The pig knows he has made the world.
Mention the possibility of something beyond it –
He farts in your face.

The pig's deepest sty is under his skin.
His skin is elegantly clad.
The pig knows might is right.
The pig is polite.

The pig is responsible and subtle.
How can this be so?
I don't know, but I have seen the pig at work
And know the truth of what I see.

The pig has lived in me

And gone his way, snouting the muck
In the wide sty of the world.

His appetite for filth is monstrous
And he knows
There is more sustenance in filth
Than in the sweet feast at the white table
Where friends gather for a night
Talk and laugh
In a room with warm light.

The pig might enter that room
And swallow everything in sight.

But the pig's sense of timing
Is flawless.
His own throat is fat, ready to cut,
But no one will do that.
Instead, the pig will slit
Some other throat.
There will be no blood but a death,
The pig will hump into the future

Huge
Hot
Effective

His eyes darting like blackbirds for the worm
Waiting to be stabbed, plucked, gulped,
Forgotten.

And still our darling lives
As though there were no
Oblivion.

The Loud Men

And how O God shall we learn to cope
With the loud men?

Yes, you have a point to make
But must you turn your fisheyes on me
As though you were the voice of revelation
And I a thing of stone?
Must you glare like a ghoul in nightmare?
Poke your burning head at me?
Spit in my face?

All I am allowed to see
Is the hysterical foam on your lips,
Your coronal of victory.

Today, in the city,
I saw a child sitting at a bridge.
Her name was Sheila Lehane.
When I spoke to her she whispered.
She had her problem.
Her voice was low and steady.

Her suffering would not allow her
To be loud.

Only bullies shout
And politicians
And bitches with phoney convictions
And bored, truculent men.
A shouting woman, however,
Is the worst of all,
A loud deformity of nature,
An articulate obscenity.

Why do they shout, I ask myself.

Because
Under the noise
There is nothing.

Because
The loud will always win attention
For a while.
Because
They are afraid of silence.
Because
They proclaim their own emptiness.
Because
By spitting in the eyes of others
They run like madmen from themselves.

When I hear a shout
I fear for humankind.

I see a black abyss
Where souls roll and writhe.

I get hell's smell, I know hell's loss,
I feel hell's evil heat.

I walk the other side of the street.

The Big Words

The first time I heard
Transubstantiation
My head fell off.

'Explain it,' the teacher said.
I looked around the classroom
Searching for my severed head
And found it near a mouse-hole
Where we used to drop
Crumbs of bread
Turning to turds
Twice as transcendental
As holy words.

'Explain it to me,' I said to my father.

From behind the great spread pages of *The Irish Independent*
'It's a miracle,' he said,
'I'm reading John D. Hickey on the semi-final
But come back later and we'll see
What's happening to Gussie Goose and Curly Wee.'

I found out what *Transubstantiation* meant.
I trotted out my answer
But the trot turned into a gallop
And I found myself witnessing a race
Between all the big words
Used by all the small men.
I use them myself, of course,
Especially when I have nothing to say,
When I cannot raise dust or hackles, go to town, or make hay
With the little bit of life in my head
Suggesting I should drink the best wine,
Eat the best bread
And thus, with a deft flick of my mind,
Transfigure the blackest hours
On this most holy ground
Where some would make their god
Hide behind big words,
Shields to stop him showing the colour of his blood
And be safe as the bland masters of jargon
Whose blindness is an appetite
For whacking great vocabularies
That cough resoundingly
In some bottomless pit
Of self-importance.

Some night soon, I'm going to have a party
For all the big words.
By the light of a semantic moon
I'll turn the race into a dance,
And with my little words
Both hosts and servants
Catering beyond their best
For even the teeniest need
Of every resonant guest,
Big and small will all be thrilled to see
Exactly what has happened
To Gussie Goose and Curly Wee

Tail-End Charlie

Tail-end Charlie
Eighteen years of age
Last of the patrol
Was ringed by women's rage

In Leeson Street
Two girls ran
To fetch the executioners
Of this young Yorkshireman

Tail-end Charlie
Could have shot his way out
But the women ringed him
He didn't shoot

Came the IRA
They did the job
On tail-end Charlie
The women went home

He had six weeks training
In the North of England
Was sent straightaway
To the North of Ireland

On his first day of duty
Lost touch with his patrol
Tail-end Charlie
Was somebody's fool

Born in black Leeds
Where life is made of smoke
Died in black Belfast
Where life is no joke

All his mothers circled him
Screaming such and such
Tail-end Charlie
Out of touch O out of touch

Blame

The devil is always blaming someone.
Bricks of blame pave the floor of hell.
The girls are cold, the horses lost in the mountains
And truth is bleeding at the bottom of the well.

De Valera at Ninety-Two

To sit here, past my ninetieth year,
Is a joy you might find hard to understand.
My wife is dead. For sixty years
She stood by me, although I know
She always kept a secret place in her heart
For herself. This I understood. There must always be
A secret place where one can go
And brood on what cannot be thought about
Where there is noise and men and women.

Some say I started a civil war.
There are those who say I split the people.
I did not.
The people split themselves.
They could not split me.
I think now I was happiest when I taught
Mathematics to teachers in their training.
From nineteen hundred and six to nineteen sixteen
I taught the teachers.
Then the trouble started.
In jail, I often sat for hours
Especially at evening
Thinking of those mathematical problems

I loved to solve.
Here was a search for harmony,
The thrill of difficulty,
The possibility of solution.
Released from jail, I set about
Making a nation,
A vicious business,
More fools among my friends than in my enemies,
Devoted to what they hardly understood.
Did I understand? You must understand
I am not a talker, but a listener.
Men like to talk, I like to listen.
I store things up inside.
I remember what many seem to forget.
I remember my grandfather
Telling of his brother's burial in Clare.
The dead man was too tall
To fit an ordinary grave
So they had to cut into a neighbour's plot,
Break the railings round a neighbour's grave
To bury a tall man.
This led to war between the families,
Trouble among the living
Over a patch o' land for the dead.
The trouble's still there. Such things, as you know,
Being a countryman yourself,
Are impossible to settle.
When my grandfather scattered things on the kitchen floor
He used strange words from the Gaelic.
I wonder still about the roots of words.
They don't teach Latin in the schools now.
That's bad, that's very bad.
It is as important to know
Where the words in your mouth come from
As where you come from yourself.
Not to know such origins
Is not to know who you are
Or what you think you're saying.
I had a small red book at school,
'Twas full of roots,
I still remember it.

Roots...and crops. Origins...and ends.
The woman who looks after me now
Tells me to sip my brandy.
Sometimes I forget I have a glass in my hand
And so I do what I'm told.
I have been blind for years.
I live in a world of voices
And of silence.
I think of my own people, the tall men,
Their strange words, the land
Unmoved by all our passions about it,
This land I know from shore to shore,
The Claremen roaring their support
And all the odds and ends
(What was that word he had for them?)
Scattered on my grandfather's kitchen floor.

Points of View

A neighbour said De Valera was
As straight as Christ,
As spiritually strong.
The man in the next house said
'Twas a great pity
He wasn't crucified as young.

Calling the Shots

He was half a mile from the road, in the fields,
When they shot him from a moving truck.
He fell like a collapsing scarecrow.
They didn't bother to stop
But took the first turn

Right and pressed on,
Having a village to burn.
The grass accommodated a dead man.
He lay there
Long enough to leave his shape in the grass
Like a resting hare.

I got the loan of a rifle from Danny King
Who loved wild geese.
I knelt by a paling-post and barbed wire
And fired at a seagull in the mud.
He fell like a doll knocked from a mantelpiece.
The incoming tide lifted a wing like paper
Shuffled by the wind.

I never met the man in the fields.
I hear he was clearing scutch.
I wonder if the soldier laughed or shuddered
Or simply forgot. Was he practising
His art? Did anyone congratulate
Him on being so accurate
From such a difficult position?
I won't forget
The seagull's wing lifting in the lazy tide
Like a hand in blessing
Moments after the shot.

The Black Fox, Again

Sixteen years ago, I saw the black fox
For what seemed the first and only time.
But last night it came back.
There was a countryman, a beggar,
Sitting on the floor behind a hall-door
Drinking whiskey from a tin-cup
Chained through a hole in the side of his mouth

Crying his eyes down and out
Because he knew he would never again know
Who or where he was.
He had beautiful slim wrists
But his face had gone dirty and cruel
With broken, red eyes
And when he said 'Give me a pound now
Because you'll be giving it to yourself'
I gave him what money I had
And felt myself unburdened of myself.
'Turn around now,' he said, 'And look
At the corner of the half-empty shed.
If you don't look, I'll wish you dead.'
I did.
There was the black fox
Back from eternity
Fixing its quiet eyes on me
But more indolent than before,
Less consciously magnificent, more piercing
And wise in the way it looked at me.
'Why have you come back?' I asked
'And why do you look at me like that?'
The black fox did not speak
But moved its eyes and sides
And I knew the dogs were coming
In all their howling might
From all the quarters of the days and nights
To kill the black fox. That
Was the moment when the black fox smiled
As if no creature had ever been defiled
By any other
And shifting its sides in a quicker rhythm
Like an instrument played by invisible fingers
Became the beggar with the face of a child
Who had no fear, for the time being,
Of dogs tamed or wild.
The dogs flocked, the beggar-child played
With heads and necks and fangs and tails
Then drove them into the shed
With a word I scarcely heard
And locked it.

As the bolt homed
Like a final thought in any simple head
The black fox faced me again,
Directed me to the hall-door
Where the young man with the cruel face
And the broken, red eyes
Complained and drank, drank and complained.
The tin-cup, chained to him,
Was always full, always drained.
The dogs were howling now.
My eyes sank deep into the black fox's eyes,
Saw dogs and chains and children and killings,
Long streets with pavements made of cries
Of those who'd journeyed far to their despair,
Deliberate women inventing faces
They might live in for a scented while,
Old men shuffling out of themselves
In frayed gaberdines of pain
Into scarce patches of sunlight
Like fresh-minted pennies, glittering.

The black fox,
Quiet, indolent and wise, went round
The far corner of the shed and vanished.
I was back out of its eyes.
The young man vanished too
Rattling his cup and chain.
The dogs had turned to silence.
The shed had no door.
The bolt had failed to become a shadow.
I shivered a little, feeling the emptiness
Wrap itself about me
Like a cold embrace
Of fingers reaching from a lost
Forbidden place.

The House That Jack Didn't Build

In the beginning was my house, Jack said,
And my house was good.
And I was in my house
And outside my house there was nothing.
And the light moved through my house
Until it was my house
So that I was made to see
Myself
Master
Of other people's houses, made from darkness
And my light shone in their darkness
But their darkness could not comprehend it.
And I willed my light to brighten all their houses.
Inspiration being my common condition
I had this divine idea.
I walked in and took them.

There was this little house
Nicely situated on the side of a hill
Within walking distance of the sea.
The moment I saw it I said to myself,
That's mine. That house was built for me.

So I walked in.

The occupant kicked up a stink.
Who do you think
You are, he asked.

I'm Jack, I said. I like houses.
I collect them.
Yours pleases me well.
A crime, you say? Nice word, crime.
You'll admire my light in time.

One can't imagine
How much I improved that house.
To start with, the garden was a mess.
He'd let it run wild.

I tamed it, gave it the sort of symmetry
Which is a perfect expression
Of the civilised mind.
Eden is what I build, not what I find.
It cost me the honest sweat of my brow.
There's not a weed there now.
I changed all the rooms.
This took me quite a while.
Visitors comment on their style.
It's simple. I do everything well,
Not exactly, to be fair, in a spirit of love
But with a genuine desire to improve
Others, particularly.

One thing worries me, though.
The former occupant won't go
Away.
He has found a small place in the hills,
A cave, or something like that.
Sometimes I hear him
Skulking outside at night
Staring at my little house
Here on the side of the hill
Within walking distance of the sea.
He's a moody brute and might kill
Me if he got the chance.
Why is he not content
To be?

I am taking all necessary precautions
Though I am bored by complaints
And plans for vengeance.
On the other hand
He might just learn to understand
And appreciate my superior position.
Yes, I'm sure he would, if he but studied my face.
Still, I don't really trust cave-dwellers.
They smell.
It's a disgrace.

I like this little place
And intend to keep it.

It's as near to perfect as I can get it.

If you saw it, I'm sure you'd agree.

It contains so much of me.

Statement of the Former Occupant

Up here in the hills
Rain rules most of the time.
Darkness drips like blood
In the cave where I live
With bats and rats and skulking shadows.

I have lost touch with my own language.
Nothing is stranger to me than what is my own.
I am an exile from myself.
Words are stones in my mouth.
The bones of my head are trampled on.

And the stink!
Since I took to living in this cave
I reek like a corpse in a grave.

Head down, shoulders bent,
Eyes stuck to clay and rock,
Words slung like corpses across my back,
I mumble

Jack
Walked in, took over my house,
Drove me to this,
Smiling Jack
Civilising Jack
Mannerly Jack
Language-changing Jack
Smooth and fluent Jack

Collector of homes, lover
Of other men's gardens.

Improver.

One day, I shall improve you, Jack.

When I improve you
I shall improve myself,
Drag myself up from the mire
To share in your glory,
Free myself from my stinking pit
To savour your exquisite order,
Abandon this daft mumbling
To achieve your eloquence,
Quit my pigsty behaviour
To emulate your manners.

I may even learn to love myself again.
A rare thing among men.

Don't be disturbed
If you see me skulking
Near your house that was once my house
And may be my house again.

Don't be upset
At assaults on your sleep
Destruction of property
Barbarous uses of language
Some shedding of blood.

Don't be dismayed.
I'm aware of the progress you've made,
The excellence you create.
It's just that I'm not mad about
Gardens that seem too neat.
Even as a child
I loved my garden
Slightly wild.
Although you've made the rooms
More elegant than I can say

It's not my way.

I am, you might say, driven,
An impassioned simpleton
Someone to look down on
Someone to joke about.
And yet
I do not seem to fear
Prison
Gallows
Rack.

Dear Jack, one day
You'll give me back my house

Though now I mumble
And even among my friends
The bats, the rats, the fickle shadows,
I go despised and broke.

On with the joke.

The Joke

Only a few alert stars
Could see the joke forming
On the lips of God.

It grew and grew
Like a spitbubble
That burst over the world,
A black rain of laughter
On parched hearts.

One man stopped another in the street and said
'Did ya hear this one?
It's a bloody howl.
All about a stupid man.'

They were so twisted with laughter
They couldn't see each other.

It was so funny
They would never forget it
For love or money.

And they told it and told it and told it
Because it was funny so funny so funny.

Paddy Taffy Limey Pole Kerryman Black Jew
And all their women too
Believe in a God
As funny as you.
His prize creation must make Him feel blue.
Yahoo!
Who?

You.
Me too.

And so it came to pass
That when he heard the joke
He was back in a parody of catechism class.

Question: Who made the world?
Answer: A little pig
              With his tail curled.
Question: What is the definition
              Of the ultimate Kerryman?
Answer: A Corkman
              Who fucks pigs.

Dear Audience, to cope with narrative problems
In a shifting context, all we must do
Is change Corkman and Kerryman
To Arab and Jew.
In this world of lies, at least that much is true!

When he made love, he wore two contraceptives
To be sure to be sure.
When he listened to sport on the radio

He burned his ear.
If you wanted to touch his mind
You put your hand on his bum.
And you knew all the time
(To laugh is no crime)
The joke made you a very bright boy
And him – stupid old scum,
A stick of ridicule beating reality's drum,

Be dumb
Be dumb

Be dumb be dumb be dumb

The joke was a sly courtier,
It flattered the King's ear.

The joke knew how to kill.
Flatter and kill, flatter and kill
The black rain sang
As it fell
Into minds, into hearts,
Over land and sea,
Over you and me.

Spill me, spill me, the black rain sang,
Tell me, tell me, tell me again,
I'm a good laugh, good laugh, good laugh.

I will lessen your pain.

The joke is growing and growing
And now there's no knowing
How it all began,

The sneer on the lips of God,
The spit of contempt on the world,
The laugh of the bright, sad man.

FROM
CROMWELL

A POEM

Note

This poem tries to present the nature and implications of various forms of dream and nightmare, including the nightmare of Irish history. Just as Irish history is inextricably commingled with English history, so is this poem's little hero, M.P.G.M. Buffún Esq., helplessy entangled with Oliver Cromwell as the latter appears and disappears in history, biography, speeches, letters, legend, folklore, fantasy, etc.

The method of the poem is imagistic, not chronological. This seemed to be the most effective way to represent a "relationship" that has produced a singularly tragic mess.

Because of history, an Irish poet, to realise himself, must turn the full attention of his imagination to the English tradition. An English poet committed to the same task need hardly give the smallest thought to things Irish. Every nightmare has its own logic.

History, however, is only a part of this poem. Buffún's nightmare is his own. Hence the fact that he is not a voice; he is many voices.

I wish to acknowledge my debt to Thomas Carlyle's *Oliver Cromwell's Letters And Speeches: With Elucidations* (five volumes, London, 1871); Christopher Hill's *God's Englishman: Oliver Cromwell and the English Revolution* (Pelican, 1970); C.H. Firth's *Cromwell's Army* (Methuen and Co, 1902); Denis Murphy's *Cromwell in Ireland* (M.H. Gill and Son, Dublin, 1883); Merle D'Aubigné's *The Protector* (Oliver and Boyd, Edinburgh, no date on my copy); W.E.H. Lecky's *A History of Ireland in the Eighteenth Century* (London, 1892); Manuscripts of *Depositions of 1641* in the Library of Trinity College, Dublin; Dorothy MacArdle's *Tragedies of Kerry* (Dublin, 1924); and various accounts, mainly in the provincial newspapers and from the conversations of survivors, and of the survivors of survivors, of the Civil War in Ireland, but chiefly in Kerry where it was said to be especially vile, 'a dirty end to a glorious fight'.

The selection here presents only a small sampling from *Cromwell*. The book itself, consisting of 254 poems, is published separately by Bloodaxe Books.

Measures

It was just that like certain of my friends I, Buffún, could not endure the emptiness. They took the measures open to them. I invited the butcher into my room and began a dialogue with him, suspecting that he'd follow a strict path of self-justification. Imagine the surprise when, with an honesty unknown to myself (for which God be thanked officially here and now) he spoke of gutted women and ashen cities, hangings and lootings, screaming soldiers and the stratagems of corrupt politicians with a cool sadness, a fluent inevitable pity. But I wasn't going to let that fool me. So, from a mountain of indignant legends, bizarre history, demented rumours and obscene folklore, I accused the butcher not merely of following the most atrocious of humanity's examples (someone was sneezing and shouting 'Mary' outside my room) but also of creating precedents of such immeasurable vileness that his name, when uttered on the lips of the unborn a thousand years hence, would ignite a rage of hate in the hearts of even the most tolerant and gentle. Imagine, I said, to create, deliberately, a name like that for yourself, to toil with such devotion towards your own immortal shame, to elect to be the very source of a tradition of loathing, the butt of jibing, despising millions. (I was really riding the old rhetoric now.)

The butcher calmly replied that the despising millions were simply millions; he was one. One. Yes, I agreed, one who makes Herod look like a benevolent Ballsbridge dad frolicking with his offspring in Herbert Park. I would remind you, returned the butcher, that you invited me here. I am the guest of your imagination, therefore have the grace to hear me out; I am not altogether responsible for the fact that you were reared to hate and fear my name which in modesty I would suggest is not without its own ebullient music. I say further that you too are blind in your way, and now you use me to try to justify that blindness. By your own admission you are empty also. So you invited me to people your emptiness. This I will do without remorse or reward. But kindly remember that you are blind and that I see.

The butcher walked out the door of my emptiness, straight into me.

Balloons

Friends beat me up on the way home from school.
Suddenly, a new time happened in me.
It wasn't that I'd come the rough or acted the fool
Too much for them to bear, it was more that they
Needed a victim that June afternoon
When you had to clamp your mouth against the flies
Cancering the air. Since then, I hate June
Because both my hips, under the bruises,
Stopped growing. In the orthopaedic hospital
I'm in the next bed to this Indian
Who can hardly be moved but a bone breaks;
My moon-faced brother looms, his pockets all
Balloons. Weights on my legs, promising man-
hood, suggesting they're the colours of mistakes.

A Friend of the People

'Mine was the first Friend's face Ireland ever saw,
Little as it recognised me,' Oliver said.
'I came equipped with God's Fact, God's Law.
What did I find? Not men but hordes
Full of hatred, falsity and noise,
Undrilled, unpaid, driving herds of plundered
Cattle before them for subsistence;
Rushing down from hillsides, ambuscadoes,
Passes in the mountains, taking shelter in bogs
Where cavalry could not follow them;
Murder, pillage, conflagration, excommunication,
Wide-flowing blood, bluster high as heaven,
Demons, rabid dogs, wolves. I brought all to heel
Yet my reward was sibylline execration.

Glancing now at my bundle of Irish letters
(A form I think I have perfected)
I see a land run by Sanguinary Quacks
Utterly unconscious of their betters.
Do you think this disease could be cured
By sprinkling it with rose-water
Like a gift of perfume to a flowering daughter?
What could I do with individuals
Whose word was worthless as the barking of dogs?
I addressed the black ravening coil
Of blusterers at Drogheda and elsewhere:

"In this hand, the laws of earth and heaven:
In this, my sword. Obey and live. Refuse and die."

They refused. They died. These letters are fire,
The honest chronicle of my desire,
Rough, shaggy as the Numidian lion,
A style like crags, unkempt, pouring, no lie.'

Manager, Perhaps?

The first time I met Oliver Cromwell
The poor man was visibly distressed.
'Buffún,' says he, 'things are gone to the devil
In England. So I popped over here for a rest.
Say what you will about Ireland, where on
Earth could a harassed statesman find peace like
This in green unperturbed oblivion?
Good Lord! I'm worn out from intrigue and work.
I'd like a little estate down in Kerry,
A spot of salmon-fishing, riding to hounds.
Good Lord! The very thought makes me delighted.
Being a sporting chap, I'd really love to
Get behind one of the best sides in the land.
Manager, perhaps, of Drogheda United?'

Rebecca Hill

Half-hanging is the rage in Kildare
It is the rebels' will
So died Jonas Wheeler William Dandy James Benn
Rebecca Hill

Rebecca Hill was fifteen years
Half-hanged then taken down
As comely a girl as ever walked
Through Kildare Town

Taken half-hanged from an oak-tree
She seemed to recover her wits
The rebels saw her flutter alive
Then buried her quick

Leaves of the oak-tree still
Flutter like Rebecca Hill.

Some People

Elizabeth Birch had a white neck
They roped it
George Butterwick of the strong body
Looked awkward naked
Sylvanus Bullock liked riding the highway
Died stripped in a ditch
John Dawling a brave swimmer
Drowned thrown off Belturbet bridge
George Netter a providing father
Perished with his five starved children
Philip Lockington a big farmer
Was flogged to an idiot beggar
Oliver Pinder offered shelter to people of the road
His house was pulled down over his head

May the Lord have mercy on the dead.

Wine

William of Orange barged into the room
In *Sunnyside* where Cromwell was resting
After chasing a fox from Mitchelstown
To Caherciveen, in vain. 'What's cooking?'
Barked Oliver, 'Why horse in here like that?
My bones are coming asunder after that chase
And the bloody fox escaped. Too much art
For these Irish hounds. But, William, what's this
Distress I see written across your face?'
'Oliver,' sweated William, 'I'm back from the Boyne
Where I drank deep draughts from victory's cup.
And yet, doubt chews my heart, I must confess.'

'Why should it?' queried Oliver.
                                        'Where's the wine?'
Croaked William, 'I think I've fucked things up!'

A Bit of a Swap

When the Pope came to Ireland, William of Orange
Was chosen by the two Houses of Government
To talk to the Pontiff on a wide range
Of subjects. William was subtle and blunt,
The right mix for a man who'd cope with the Pope.

'Holy Father,' smiled William, mustering his intellectual forces,
'My chief concern is Irish industry. I hope
You'll like my suggestion about thoroughbred horses.
I understand you have a deep interest in bulls
And own, in fact, some choice Italian herds.
Swap bulls for horses, that's what I propose.'

The Pontiff ruminated: 'My child, your sales
In horses are about to soar. My word
On that. As for my bulls to you, who knows?'

An Example

'In Limerick, the besieged Irish were all plague and famine.
Great numbers of people tried to abandon the town,
Sent out by the garrison as useless persons
Or to spread their contagion among us. Ireton
Commanded them to go back, threatened to shoot
Any that should come out in future. This
Failed. Ireton decided we should execute
Some, an example. I chose the only full-breasted
Wench in the bunch. Her father was with her,
Begged he be hanged instead of his daughter.
I said no. 'Up on the gibbet, lass. Mount! Mount!'
I hanged her in full sight of the town walls.
The gaping townsfolk were so filled with terror
We were no longer disturbed on that account.'

A Condition

Oliver is a blunt man,
Blunter than any fiddling poet can be.
He squatted outside the town,
Wrote a letter to the Enemy.

'Surrender, you may leave this place.
Resist, you're dead. Decision by return.
If you wish to see me face to face
Come to the Mass-rock outside the town.'

The two men met there. The defender
Would capitulate on one condition.
'A condition,' he said, 'that nothing can shake.'

'What? A condition?' roared Oliver.
In the burning of an eye he grabbed the man,
Smashed his head against the Mass-rock.

164

Discipline

'You know your Irish tragedy, Buff?' queried
Oliver, 'It's this: you have no discipline.
Discipline cannot be rushed or hurried
But is a problem of moulding men to my vision
Of them. Can an Irishman be properly moulded?
Your common Englishman can, admirably so.
I moulded an army of disciplined soldiers.
They fought well. When the day came for them to go
Back to the world, they kept their discipline.
Of all that army, not a man begged in the streets.
This captain turned shoemaker, this lieutenant a baker,
This a brewer, that a haberdasher,
This common soldier, a porter; each man in his
Frock and apron, disciplined, an English worker.'

Oliver's Prophecies

'I will be remembered as a killer of language,
As Coppernose, Rubynose, Nose Almighty.
Before the battle of Worcester, in a fit of rage,
I will sign a pact with the Devil
Using the blood from the little finger
Of my right hand. He will give me seven years
To do my work. I'll do it. I'll be the centre
Of blame, the heartbeat of hate, the focus of fear.
I'll stable horses in St Canice's Cathedral,
I'll be a farmer, a brewer, a shoemaker,
I'll have a portrait of the Devil on the wall
Of my bedroom. Each night, exhausted, I
Will pass the portrait. It will smile and bow and say
"Dear Noll, we'll never part company".'

A Relationship

'Cromwell,' I said, 'If our relationship
Is to develop, there's something I must tell
You, something from which I can't escape.
I hate and fear you like the thought of hell.
The murderous syllables of your name
Are the foundation of my nightmare.
I can never hate you enough. That is my shame.
Every day I pray that I may hate you more.
A fucked-up Paddy is what I am. Right?
Wrong. My loathing is such I know
I'll never rest.'

Oliver smiled. 'I sympathise with your plight,
Buffún. Understandable. You're fine, though, so
Long as you get it off your chest.'

'You really are an understanding
Son-of-a-bitch, Oliver,' I replied
'And when this nightmare is over
And I understand why I have hated
You, your language, your army and your Christ
Who suffers your puritan crap
When he should bleed your guts into the sun
Or rip your heart out or break your neck
Or manacle you forever to a rock
Or stuff the barrel of a gun
Up your arse or assassinate your prick

Then we shall sit together
Outside a pub on a June afternoon
Sipping infinite pints of cool beer.
I have been brooding on this, mulling it over,
Our destinies are mingled, late and soon.
But the prospects are not good, I fear.'

Nails

The black van exploded
Fifty yards from the hotel entrance.
Two men, one black-haired, the other red,
Had parked it there as though for a few moments
While they walked around the corner
Not noticing, it seemed, the children
In single file behind their perky leader,
And certainly not seeing the van
Explode into the children's bodies.
Nails, nine inches long, lodged
In chest, ankle, thigh, buttock, shoulder, face.
The quickly-gathered crowd was outraged and shocked.
Some children were whole, others bits and pieces.
These blasted crucifixions are commonplace.

'Therefore, I Smile'

'Under it all,' Oliver said, 'The problem was simple.
How could I make Ireland work?
The Irish hate work, not knowing what it means.
I do. Work exists. It is inevitable and stark,
A dull, fierce necessity. Later ages may consider it
Superfluous but my glimpses of this world were true.
I looked, I saw, I considered, I did what
Was necessary. To live is to work. To be is to do.

Put a man in a field
A soldier fighting a wall
A wife in bed
A whore in a street
A king on a throne

Someone must dig a grave for the dead
And the dead must rot.

Even dead flesh works in the earth
But not the Irish, Buff, not you, not your countrymen.
They will prattle, argue, drink, yarn, but not
Work. Someone had to teach them
Not to idle their lives away.
I taught them to do things my way.
Against their will
I gave them a style.
I tendered them the terrible gift of my name,
Knowing they would make songs about me
Echoing curses soaked in verbal bile
Twisted poems and stories
To make me an excuse for what they
Would fail to do, to be, being themselves.

I am Oliver Cromwell still.

Therefore, I smile.'

A Running Battle

What are they doing now? I imagine Oliver
Buying a Dodge, setting up as a taxi-driver
Shunting three dozen farmers to Listowel Races.
I see Ed Spenser, father of all our graces
In verse, enshrined as a knife-minded auctioneer
Addicted to Woodbines and Kilkenny beer,
Selling Parish Priests' shiny furniture
To fox-eyed housewives and van-driving tinkers.
William of Orange is polishing pianos
In convents and other delicate territories,
His nose purple from sipping turpentine.
Little island is Big, Big Island is little.
I never knew a love that wasn't a running battle
Most of the time. I'm a friend of these ghosts. They're mine.

Am

When I consider what all this has made me
I marvel at the catalogue:
I am that prince of liars, Xavier O'Grady,
I am Tom Gorman, dead in the bog,
I am Luke O'Shea in Limerick prison,
I sell subversive papers at a church gate,
Men astound me, I am outside women,
I have fed myself on the bread of hate,
I am an emigrant in whose brain
Ireland bleeds and cannot cease
To bleed till I come home again
To fields that are a parody of peace.
I sing tragic songs, I am madly funny,
I'd sell my country for a fist of money,
I am a big family,
I am a safe-hearted puritan
Blaming it all on the Jansenists
Who, like myself, were creatures on the run.
I am a home-made bomb, a smuggled gun.
I like to whine about identity,
I know as little of love as it is possible
To know, I bullshit about being free,
I'm a softie crying at the sound of a bell,
I have a tongue to turn snakespittle to honey,
I smile at the themes of the old poets,
Being lost in myself is the only way
I can animate my foolish wits.

Do I believe myself? I spill
My selves. Believe, me, if you will.

Index of titles and first lines

(Titles are italics. The numbers refer to pages.)

Brendan Kennelly was born in 1936 in Ballylongford, Co. Kerry, and was educated at St Ita's College, Tarbert, Co. Kerry; at Trinity College, Dublin, where he gained his BA, MA and PhD, and Leeds University. He has lectured in English Literature at Trinity College since 1963, and became its Professor of Modern Literature in 1973. He has also lectured in America where he was Guildersleeve Professor at Barnard College, New York, in 1971, and Cornell Professor of Literature at Swarthmore College, Pennsylvania, in 1971-72. He won the AE Memorial Prize for Poetry in 1967 and the Critics' Special Harveys Award in 1988.

He has published more than twenty books of poems, including *My Dark Fathers* (1964), *Collection One: Getting Up Early* (1966), *Good Souls to Survive* (1967), *Dream of a Black Fox* (1968), *Love Cry* (1972), *The Voices* (1973), *Shelley in Dublin* (1974), *A Kind of Trust* (1975), *Islandman* (1977), *A Small Light* (1979) and *The House That Jack Didn't Build* (1982). *The Boats Are Home* (1980) is still available from Gallery Press and *Moloney Up and At It* from the Mercier Press (Cork and Dublin).

His best-known work is the popular and controversial book-length poem-sequence *Cromwell*, published in Ireland by Beaver Row Press in 1983 and in Britain by Bloodaxe Books in 1987.

His books of poems translated from the Irish include *A Drinking Cup* (Allen Figgis, 1970) and *Mary* (Aisling Press, Dublin 1987), and his translations are now collected in *Love of Ireland: Poems from the Irish* (Mercier Press, 1989). He edited *The Penguin Book of Irish Verse* (1970; 2nd edition 1981), and has published two novels, *The Crooked Cross* (1963) and *The Florentines* (1967).

He is also a celebrated dramatist whose plays include versions of *Antigone*, produced at the Peacock Theatre, Dublin, in 1986, and *Medea* premièred in the Dublin Theatre Festival in 1988 and toured in England in 1989 by the Medea Theatre Company. His stage version of *Cromwell* played to packed houses at Dublin's Damer Hall in 1986 and 1987. His selection *Landmarks of Irish Drama* was published by Methuen in 1988.

His other books include *The Real Ireland*, a book of photographs by Liam Blake with text by Brendan Kennelly (Appletree Press, Belfast, 1984), and *Ireland Past and Present*, edited by Brendan Kennelly (Chartwell Books, New Jersey, 1985).

He has published five volumes of selected poems: *Selected Poems* (Allen Figgis, 1969), *Selected Poems* (Dutton, New York, 1971), *New and Selected Poems* (Gallery Press, 1976), *Selected Poems* (Kerrymount, Dublin, 1985), and *A Time for Voices: Selected Poems 1960-1990* (Bloodaxe Books, 1990). His latest book-length sequence, *Judas*, is published by Bloodaxe Books in 1991.